I Want To Be "Left Behind"

Book One in the "I Want To Be Left Behind" series

I Want To Be "Left Behind"

An Examination of the Ideas Behind the
Popular Series and the End Times

Tim Kirk

Writers Club Press
San Jose New York Lincoln Shanghai

I Want To Be "Left Behind"
An Examination of the Ideas Behind the Popular Series and the End Times

All Rights Reserved © 2002 by Timothy Kirk

Writers Club Press
an imprint of iUniverse, Inc.

For information address:
iUniverse, Inc.
5220 S. 16th St., Suite 200
Lincoln, NE 68512
www.iuniverse.com

ISBN: 0-595-22427-X

Printed in the United States of America

Dedicated to Catherine,
"The Bestest in the whole wide world."

Eschatology (Es·cha·tol·o·gy):

A study concerning the end of creation as we know it, or of orthodox Christian doctrines regarding the second coming of Jesus Christ, the final judgment of men, and the resurrection of the dead.

Contents

Foreword

You ever notice how the last of anything is important? Take bread for example: no one cares about bread until you've made half a peanut butter and jelly sandwich and realize you don't have another piece of bread. Sometimes its the epiphany that your son's third bowl of Captain Crunch means you won't have any milk left for your first cup of coffee. Occasionally the last of something is beneficial because it's a commonly understood rule that if a person asks for a piece of gum and you say, "This is my last piece," that means you aren't obligated to share.

Speaking of last things, I was introduced to the topic of eschatology the same way an introducer presents an introducee that they've forgotten the name of—very generally. In fact, I wasn't acquainted with the term "eschatology" until the gentleman whose book you are reading approached me with it. As a Christian, I knew there was going to come to pass an end-of-the-world-as-we-know-it but I had no idea what that would entail. Then I was told of a taped sermon by the pastor of the local assembly I was a member of. The sermon was his message to those that had remained after the rapture, to wit, those "Left Behind." I listened intently as the pastor spoke of terrible things that would happen to those still on this plane of existence but that there might be a glimmer of a hope for what essentially would be second-class citizens in heaven—those that had rejected the Gospel until the Great Tribulation began. Of course, you had to be a Jew and had to do so without the aid of the Holy Spirit but hey, it could happen, right?

Armed (and I do mean "armed") with that knowledge, I went on my merry way thinking I had it down. Then I ran into that word: eschatology. No longer was it a simple story about events that would happen to others (hey, I was getting raptured so what did I care). Now it was an "Ology," something that needed to be studied and under-stood. It ranked right up there with other fifty-cent words I was barely accustomed to pronouncing; words like soteriology, ecclesiology, hamartiology, and pneumatology were already tying my tongue up in knots—why not add another?

I came to recognize that much like the other "Ologies," eschatology wasn't some obscure point of study for scholars. Likewise, eschatology wasn't some sensationalist drama written in the headlines or on church billboards. No, eschatology is both much less grandiose and much more substantial to Christianity than either faction would like. Our understanding of eschatology has a dynamic effect on any Christian's ability to not only communicate the Gospel but also to understand the Gospel.

This book was written by a man who doesn't want to have the last word on the subject or have you finish his book and say, "Yeah, now I've got this down pat." I believe his greatest aspiration for this work is that it becomes a footnote in your search for Truth and your under-standing of Christ.

Thankfully, he felt obligated to share.

—**Raymond F. Pomerico II**
The Macon Telegraph
Macon, GA

Preface

I didn't mean to write a book. I really mean it. I never wanted to. I never looked to be an author of any kind because I am everything authors aren't. I am a procrastinator. I always wait until the night (or sometimes, the hour) before papers are due in school. I don't know any authors, though there are many I find fascinating, and would love to meet. (Well, I take that back. My father did write a dissertation for a doctorate, and a friend of mine once met Tom Clancy and didn't like him). I guess if I met my favorite authors, there's a chance I'd be disappointed, too.

So, why did I write this? I admit I am reluctant even now as I type. My father always warned me against writing books. He said, "you should be ashamed to let anyone read anything you have written before 10 years from the day you wrote it." He's a smart guy, and it hasn't been 10 years yet…shame on me.

I wrote this book because so many people have adopted the "Left Behind" theology. Is that bad? No, it is not. The "Left Behind" view is orthodox and falls within the pale of several acceptable views. Is it good, then? No, I don't think so. While the view is acceptable theologically, there is a deeper matter at hand. That deeper matter is precisely why I took to writing this. My point of view might surprise you, anger you, or even make you stop reading this (but no one ever reads the preface, so I press on without fear)!

I am not a clergyman. I am not a professor. I have nothing to sell. In fact my sincere hope is that this book came to you free of charge (if not, it does carry a money-back guarantee if it fails to challenge your thinking ;-). My only hope is to open minds, charge conversation, and to springboard the debate within the church over this very important matter of "the end times." My purpose is to, dare I say, rebut the notions put forth by Mr. LaHaye. I wish to do so respectfully, humbly, and with a tenor glorifying to Christ.

I don't come from any traditional category of interpretation. If you must label these ideas, my teachers come from a variety of backgrounds: R.C. Sproul, Josh McDowell, Chuck Swindoll, Hank Hanegraaff, Ken Gentry, and Dr.'s Jim Covey and Norman Geisler. I guess we'll call it Bapticalvinistic Apologetical Evangelism. Sounds cool, huh?

This is not meant to settle the issue of eschatology. My point in all this is simply to lay out an argument disputing some of the popular assertions of the "Left Behind" doctrine. Why? I do so for the sake of sound interpretation of scripture for the purpose of rightly dividing the word. This work is an invitation to the reader. I am going to hit you with quotations from scholars that'll make you THINK about scripture. I am going to hit you with a hermeneutic (process of interpretation of scripture) that uses scripture to interpret scripture. I invite you to carefully consider the Word of God and what it has to say. At the very least, this book should drive you to scripture, make you dive into it, and roll around in there until it gets all over you. If the least that happens is the reader immerses themselves in scripture in earnest, I have succeeded. Sound fun? Let's go....

Acknowledgements

Thanks to Jimmy C., Hank H., Norm G., Dwain G., RC S., and others for making me think.

Thanks to Dr. Robert Kirk for being the wisest man I know, and for sharing that wisdom.

Thanks to Mom and Dad for everything…especially the sandwiches.

Thanks to Mark for being the "Best Man" around.

Thanks to the Navs for the sharpening.

Thanks to the Zoo for making it burn.

Thanks to Brandon, Ray, Pete, and Mike
for the Championships of 1999 and 2000.

Semper Veritas Boomer Sooner!

Introduction

They're everywhere. No matter where one looks, the "Left Behind" series of products by Tim LaHaye is sure to catch the eye. The books, tapes, CDs, and videos are found in media outlets, both Christian and secular alike. Personally, I am not surprised by the booming popularity of these products. I grew up in a Southern Baptist church in the 1970's. I still remember the waning days of the <u>Late Great Planet Earth</u> fad. As a member of a Baptist youth group in the 1980's, I was exposed time and time again to the "Thief in the Night" series of films. Of course, who could forget the explosion of "End Times" literature during the Gulf War of the early 1990's? It seems fitting to have the "Left Behind" experience follow in the footsteps of these media booms into the new millennium.

There is a slight difference this time, however. While each of the prior fads emerged in the form of a singular media form like a book or a movie, the "Left Behind" experience is a multimedia experience. The movie, once available in theaters, is now available on video. The books are available in print, cassette tape, CD, and in various "mini-versions" for specialized audiences like youth. Whether at home, in the car, or on a plane, "Left Behind's" message of doom is available to all in varied forms. This latest movement of ideas is unparalleled in exposure.

As I have been discipled, and as I disciple others, the topic always seems to come up in lessons and studies. The "Left Behind" message and the questions it addresses have emerged as a huge part of American culture. Questions like, "are we living in the last days," or "who do you think the Antichrist is," are an indelible part of Christian conversation. The impact of the "Left Behind" phenomenon is truly amazing.

Why is it so popular? Because it is absolutely sensational to read about the "End Times" in our day!! Eschatology (the study of last things) appears to be a booming part of church study. Some evangelical churches are even making eschatololgical points in their statements of faith. The impact on our thinking is enormous. Just ask yourself this question: "Would you ever allow the government to put a mark of any kind on your right hand or forehead?" Your answer will be invariably linked to your view of eschatology. That is precisely the matter at hand: your eschatology. Tim LaHaye and others want to force a particular view of eschatology on the church today. How should the church react to that? I think we can all agree on the answer to that: the church should react with noble character!

The idea of reacting with noble character comes right from scripture in the Book of Acts. We've all heard the story from Acts 17:11, and how the Bereans were of more noble character in their response to Paul's teaching than the Thessalonians were. It is a great story, and I really appreciate the rendering the New Living Translation gives the passage: "And the people of Berea were more open-minded than those in Thessalonica, and they listened eagerly to Paul's message. They searched the Scriptures day after day to check up on Paul and Silas, to see if they were really teaching the truth." Some people might object to the use of the term "open-minded," but it is referring to the fact that the Bereans didn't incite a riot when Paul started preaching. The Bereans listened, and searched the scriptures to check up on Paul. I invite the reader to do the same from this point on. Check the scriptures about Acts 17. Does your translation say "noble character?" If you want to compare translations, look at an online Bible like www.biblegateway.com, or to compare, look at the Greek, the Hebrew, the commentaries. Study, refer, and check up on me. DO NOT believe anything I say, or anything anyone else says just because they say it. The church should believe something because God has said it in His Word. We'll come back to that idea again soon.

The issue is not whether one adopts the "Left Behind" eschatology, the issue is the uncritical adoption of "Left Behind" or any other eschatology. My aim is to encourage the body to be like the Bereans. They adopted Paul's message based upon a careful consideration of his points. When the church studies eschatology, and adopts ideas and notions, it should be based on careful consideration of the teacher's points.

This book will briefly outline the major categories of eschatology interpretation, refer you to some books that go deeper into the issues, and scrutinize areas of the "Left Behind" theology to see if it really is the truth. In fact, much like the <u>Left Behind</u> series of books, this book is intended to be one of a series. The effort is to take the issues at hand in bite-sized portions, so as to keep things simple and understandable. The topic is controversial, sometimes difficult, and certainly not without complexities. The series will take things step-by-step in order to provide a clear approach to the purpose.

Keep in mind, the purpose of this series is not to persuade you to adopt or reject a particular doctrine. With one exception, of course, and that purpose is based upon scripture. Colossians 2:8 says this: "Don't let anyone lead you astray with empty philosophy and high-sounding nonsense that come from human thinking and from the evil powers of this world, and not from Christ." (NLT) The exception I refer to is the purpose of adopting ideas that come from Christ, and rejecting ideas that do not. That's a heavy notion. This examination will hold up ideas and teachings the way the Bereans did: comparing teachings and ideas with scripture to see if they are true. If any idea is true: it comes from Christ. If any idea is untrue, it comes from the world and human thinking. I am not out to get Tim LaHaye, or anybody else! I just want to encourage the body of Christ to adopt ideas that come from him based on critical analysis of His word. If that results in someone adopting the "Left Behind" ideas after critical examination, so be it! No bad feelings! The error comes from failure to examine the ideas against scripture to see if they are true. The beauty of it is: one day Christ will return the same way he left! We can rejoice in that together!

This series begins with this book: an examination of basic principles of end times study, and a look at the elementary notions of the "Left Behind" series. Specifically, we'll study the parts of scripture where the simple notion of being "Left Behind" comes from. We'll analyze the word to see if scripture points towards the conclusions of the "Left Behind" doctrine. Then we'll look at some alternatives to see if they hold up to scripture any better or worse than "Left Behind" does. By the end of this book, you'll know the following things:

What part of scripture the "Left Behind" ideas come from
How to analyze the context of that scripture
How Christians who hold other interpretations of that scripture see it
Where to go for further study of the scripture and the various interpretations

In order to address these points, we'll begin with a definition of categories of "end times" biblical interpretation. It is important to know "Left Behind" follows a certain model of interpretation. It is also important to know that it is not the only model of interpretation within the church. There are other ideas on end times that are also orthodox doctrines. These doctrines will form the basis of our examination of alternative views on the end times. Please remember, I am not trying to endorse one category over another. I admit it: I do believe certain categories have strengths over others. I also admit I do not fall into the same category as the "Left Behind" series does. I will, however, do my absolute best to remain objective. However, if I ever do sound biased, please forgive me. "See, I have told you ahead of time!" ;-) I do want to be biased, but only biased against ideas that do not come from Christ. There is a difference between bias based upon Colossians 2:8, and bias based upon loyalty to a doctrine or category of thought.

That loyalty to a doctrine or category of thought within the church is precisely what I invite the reader and myself to check at the door as we begin. Our objectivity should be based on Colossians 2:8, and Acts 17:11, and other scriptures. Our ability to compare scripture with scripture to gain understanding is exactly what will help us in this analysis. Let us begin.

1

End Times Categories of Interpretation or There's More Than One Way to Skin a Beast

The essence of this volume begins from this premise: there are several categories of end times interpretation that fall within orthodox Christianity. There are also various subcategories to each view. For more information about these categories and subcategories, reference a book called <u>Three Views on the Millennium and Beyond</u>, edited by Darrell L. Bock. Another good reference is <u>Revelation: Four Views</u>, edited by Steve Gregg. These books provide an objective examination of the categories and subcategories of end times beliefs by examining the scriptures via independent thinkers who represent their own category of thought. It is important to realize the fact that there are several valid views within Christianity. No single perspective of the following groups has a right to the claim as the "only" true Christian view. It just so happens that today there is overwhelming exposure for one particular subcategory's view, the "Left Behind" view. This has the effect of making it appear as though the "Left Behind" interpretation is the only one in existence, or that others are foreign, new, or even heretical. It is interesting to note that I can find no ancient creedal statements endorsing one position or another. So the notion of heresy with respect to eschatology appears limited to disputes about the fact of Christ's return, not the details surrounding it. The major categories must therefore be viewed as orthodox doctrine. My purpose is to open the examination with a light exposure to the major categories within church history.

For the purpose of this book, we will limit the review to the three major categories of eschatology in the church. They are identified by their perspective on a period known as "The Millennium," a time referred to indirectly in John's Revelation. The three are:

- Pre-millennialism

- Post-millennialism

- A-millennialism

(These words have their prefixes hyphenated for clarity)

The issue in dispute between these systems of interpretation is whether or not there is a real and literal 1,000 year rule of Jesus Christ on the earth, and when it might take place. Pre-millennial thinkers believe Jesus Christ will return in either a one or two phased event that ushers in a literal 1,000 year reign of Christ on earth. Post-millennial thinkers see the current church age as advancing towards (or marching through) a figurative millennial period between Christ's first and second comings. This period is marked by gradual advancement of the gospel which introduces the conditions of the millennial period. His second coming effectively ends history with a final resurrection and judgment. A-millennial thinkers reject millennialism altogether. They see the church age as a fulfillment of the millennium, with no future millennial reign of Christ on earth. When He returns, He will introduce the new heaven and earth spoken of in John's Revelation. They see the current age as a period with Christ reigning on earth by virtue of his throne and the Holy Spirit in the hearts of men. So think of it this way:

Millennium = A period of Christ's reign, either a literal 1,000-year period on earth, or a figurative period of undetermined length. It is viewed as possibly coming in the future, or present in some form today.

Pre-millennial = We are looking forward to the return of Christ to bring the millennium

Post-millennial = We are working towards or even in the millennium prior to Christ's return

A-millennial = We are living in the period referred to as millennium: the age where the Church is on earth

Sounds simple, huh? Naturally, I'm Kidding…there is nothing simple about it! The questions are vast and varied, and years of devoted study are required to cover all the issues. This leads many people to ask, "So why would God make everything so vague and confusing?" If that is you, welcome to the club!! Many of us have experienced the frustration of not understanding a particular passage. So what is the point? The point is elegant and simple: to get us into God's word. I believe God left us everything we need to live in this age; scripture is sufficient for all things in our lives. Some of the details, however, are difficult to grasp with our finite minds. God wants us to find out all about Him by finding all that is in His word: the Bible. If you find the end times topic complicated, please, PLEASE do not adopt the great cop out position:

Pan-millennialism = The belief that it will "all pan out" in the end

I know many people who joke around with that line. As a joke, it's great. As a doctrine, however, its lousy! God has given us his scripture to consume with our minds and hearts. Remember the greatest commandment? We are called to love the Lord with all our minds, as well as the rest of our being. How can we do that if we intellectually check out on an important aspect of his word? I encourage everyone to engage, don't cop out. By studying God's word on this topic, you'll learn so much more about Him in many other diverse topics, too. Trust me, there is more to it than just the details of the end times.

Back to our issues at hand: it is important to realize the fact that there are several valid views within Christianity. No single perspective of these groups has a right to the claim themselves as the "only true Christian view." It just so happens that today there is overwhelming exposure for one particular category's view, the "Left Behind" view. Their category is the pre-millennial viewpoint. This particular view is very catchy due to its futuristic context. Think of it: the idea of a coming "Big Brother" world leader who will take over everything, a mark on your hand you have to take to buy or sell, a seven-year period of earthquakes, famines, pestilence, and war concluding with the great battle of Armageddon!! Absolutely sensational reading, no? As sensational as this is, it remains important not to favor this idea simply due to its entertainment appeal. We have to carefully consider ideas and compare them with scripture to see if they come from Christ, or from the world. You'll probably never see a series of fiction books based upon an a-millennial model of events, now will you? An a-millennial version might be called The Millennium Idea—Left Behind...you think? My point is the reason for adopting one of these three constructs should not be based upon their multimedia presentation, but by their origin. Do the ideas truly come from Christ? That is for you to decide yourself. Please don't believe any doctrine just because Kirk Cameron acts it out on the big screen. Nothing against Cameron, but that would certainly not qualify as a Berean character trait.

2

The Olivet Discourse and the "End Times" or Why I Want to be Left Behind!!

The statement, "I want to be left behind!!" will certainly disturb some people. If one finds that statement upsetting or shocking, it reveals something about that person's beliefs on the "end times." The title of the book and this chapter is designed to be a bit shocking in order to grab your attention and get you thinking. The concern here is the source of the words, beliefs, and doctrine which affects our beliefs. The introduction stated one of the things this book would do is tell you what part of scripture the "Left Behind" ideas come from. The essence of this chapter is to identify the passages of scripture many "Left Behind" ideas come from, and to provide an analysis of the key points. At the end of this chapter, you will understand the title of this book a bit better, understand the context of the scripture behind the notion of "Left Behind," and understand why someone might say, "I want to be left behind!!"

The 24th Chapter of Matthew has a passage known as "The Olivet Discourse." It is known by that name because it describes a discussion, or discourse, Jesus had with his disciples on the Mount of Olives. In modern terms, it might be called a sermon or a lesson, but the name of the passage comes from tradition. The passage is also told in Mark 13 and Luke 21, but the Matthew version of events is the version many use to explain the points Jesus made—though they each tell the same story. The "discourse" delivers prophecies to the disciples about things to come. It provides the basis for many "end times" doctrines.

A complete and thorough understanding of Matthew 24 is vital to understanding any "end times" doctrine. For the purposes of this book, we will limit our analysis to the context of Matthew 24 within the book of Matthew, and specific points within Mark 13 and Luke 21 as they relate to "Left Behind" (LB) doctrine. The position of LB doctrine is that most or all of the Olivet Discourse has a future fulfillment in prophecy. Other views hold that Matthew 24 is either partially fulfilled, or completely fulfilled in history. While this is an important issue, we'll examine some smaller issues first on our way to a complete analysis in later volumes.

Matthew 24 begins with the story of the initiation of the conversation between Jesus and the disciples:

> As Jesus was leaving the Temple grounds, his disciples pointed out to him the various Temple buildings. 2. But he told them, "Do you see all these buildings? I assure you, they will be so completely demolished that not one stone will be left on top of another!"

This transaction leads to the conversation as the chapter proceeds:

> Later, Jesus sat on the slopes of the Mount of Olives. His disciples came to him privately and asked, "When will all these things take place? And will there be any sign ahead of time to signal your return and the end of the world?"

This question the disciples asked Jesus kicks off the discourse. Jesus' answer to the question forms the discourse. Notice the essence of the disciple's question is:

When will all these things happen?

Are there any signs to signal these things happening?

Understanding the question is almost as important as understanding the answer. We can't understand the answer to a question if we don't get the question. To understand the question, we have to clearly see the context of the question. Notice the disciples point out the buildings of the temple to Jesus. Why did they do that? Then they ask when will "all" these things happen. What do they mean, "all these things?" The context of the question clears the picture.

It is unwise to build a doctrine on a single verse without considering the context of the verse. It is also unwise to build a doctrine on a single chapter without considering the context of the chapter or passage. For the context of the opening lines of Mathew 24, we should look at the passage preceding it, namely Matthew 23. Matthew 23 is one of the most powerful passages of scripture, and contains one of the toughest (if not the toughest) confrontations Jesus ever had with the Jewish leaders. Portions of this confrontation contain words of Jesus that might lead the disciples to ask the questions recorded in Matthew 24. For instance:

> 23:33 Snakes! Sons of vipers! How will you escape the judgment of hell? 34 I will send you prophets and wise men and teachers of religious law. You will kill some by crucifixion and whip others in your synagogues, chasing them from city to city.

Here Jesus tells the Jewish leaders they are snakes, sons of vipers, and condemned to hell. He also refers to the disciples when he explains that the Jews will murder wise teachers and prophets sent to them. Other disciples who escape death will be whipped or chased all across the land. No doubt this notion did not escape the disciples' attention! They undoubtedly would be interested in when these things would happen, and if there were signs to precede them. If you heard from the Lord of the universe that you would be sent out to teach and the people you were sent to would most likely murder you or chase you out of town, what would you say? Think about that as Jesus continues his remarks to the Jewish leaders:

23:35 As a result [of murdering Jesus and his disciples], you will become guilty of murdering all the godly people from righteous Abel to Zechariah son of Barachiah, whom you murdered in the Temple between the altar and the sanctuary. 36 I assure you, all the accumulated judgment of the centuries will break upon the heads of this very generation.

Let me repeat verse 36 for emphasis:

I assure you [speaking to the Jewish leaders], all the accumulated judgment of the centuries will break upon the heads of this very generation.

Wow. Can you imagine? God the Son declares the Jews will murder him and some of his disciples, and further declares that as a result, the Jews will become guilty of the murder of EVERY godly person literally from A to Z. Abel to Zechariah. Their punishment? "All the accumulated judgment of the centuries" will fall upon the Jews. I find the words of the people of Jerusalem frightening later on in Matthew 27 as they choose to crucify Jesus and release Barabbas:

27:24…[Pilate said] "I am innocent of the blood of this man. The responsibility is yours!"
27:25 And all the people yelled back, "We will take responsibility for his death—we and our children!"

So let us consider this: Jesus declares the Jewish leaders are snakes, and that they will incur the guilt of the centuries by killing him and others, and that the judgment for that will fall upon that very generation. Further down the line in scripture, the people accept full responsibility (on themselves AND their children) for Jesus' death at the judgment seat of Pilate. Jesus concludes Matthew 23 by weeping for Jerusalem, and announces that the house of Jerusalem has been left to them desolate. At this point in scripture, Matthew 24 begins, and the disciples approach Jesus as he leaves the temple.

Keep in mind Jesus' exchange with the Jewish leaders in Matthew 23 took place at the temple. So as he is leaving that confrontation, the disciples want to talk with him about what he just said:

> 24:1 As Jesus was leaving the Temple grounds, his disciples pointed out to him the various Temple buildings.

It is hard to imagine the disciples pointing out the buildings in a casual way, isn't it? Mark 13 and Luke 21 make the conversation sound more casual, and one might conclude the observations were, in fact almost bragging about the great temple they had. That is a true possibility. Considering all that just took place in Matthew 23, I personally doubt their comments were simply casual and boastful. They must have understood the announcement of Jerusalem's house (the temple) being left desolate, and the implications of a judgment so intense as to include the accumulated judgment of the centuries all the way back to Abel. I assume their pointing out of the temple buildings was at least indirectly related to the announcements Jesus made in chapter 23.

Jesus declares that not one stone will be left on top of another in the temple complex. That had to be upsetting to a group of faithful Jews like the disciples. Remember, the temple was the center of their world. The temple housed the Holy of Holies, the sacrifice for sins, and the ritual implements for man's reconciliation to God. For it to be completely demolished would truly be devastating. Look at their questions in Matthew 24, Mark 13, and Luke 21:

> Matthew 24:3 "…When will all this take place? And will there be any sign ahead of time to signal your return and the end of the world (age)?"

> Mark 13:4 "When will all this take place? And will there be any sign ahead of time to show us when all this will be fulfilled?"

Luke 21:7 "…When will all this take place? And will there be any sign ahead of time?"

When one reads Matthew 24, one might think the question was related to the physical destruction of the world itself: the literal end of time. However, Mark 13 and Luke 21 do not carry the same connotation. Based upon these other verses, the question sounds more like a reference to the destruction of the temple as a part of the judgment on the Jews (not to mention their own deaths mentioned in Matthew 23). Keep in mind, to a group of devoted Jews like the disciples, the destruction of the temple ranked right next to the end of the world! But notice, too, the translation of Matthew 24 is also rendered with the word "age" in the footnotes. In light of the other parallel verses, one could favor the interpretation of "age" safely within the context of the rest of scripture.

So their question boils down to: "when is the temple going to be destroyed, what signs will indicate that it is about to happen?" Everything that follows in the Olivet Discourse should be viewed as an answer to their question. Historically, the temple was destroyed by the Romans in the year 70 AD. The Olivet Discourse took place between 30 and 40 AD give or take a year. So Jesus predicted the temple's destruction, and it took place 30-40 years later. That generation and their children took the hit. He was right on.

The rest of the chapter is open to debate as to the details and what is meant by each passage. We will examine these details in later volumes, but for now, we'll stick to two particulars. One particular we'll save for the next chapter. The other point we'll examine here: the issue of being "Left Behind." Where does the phrase or even the idea come from? If the reader is at all familiar with the LB message, the notion of being left anywhere comes from the notion of the church being taken away by Jesus to be with God in a dramatic event called, "The Rapture."

The word, "Rapture" never appears in scripture. However portions of the Olivet Discourse provide the backdrop for the idea of a rapture, and being left behind:

> 24:40 "Two men will be working together in the field; one will be taken, the other left. 41 Two women will be grinding flour at the mill; one will be taken, the other left. 42 So be prepared, because you don't know what day your Lord is coming."

Sounds rapture-esque, doesn't it? However, look carefully at the preceding verses:

> 24:37 "When the Son of Man returns, it will be like it was in Noah's day.

Many people use this as an argument for the notion that world events will get worse and worse, right up to the level of Noah's day (In Noah's day, Noah and his family were the only righteous people on earth). However that idea of things getting worse and worse towards the end is not from Christ's illustration. The Lord continues:

> 38 In those days before the Flood, the people were enjoying banquets and parties and weddings right up to the time Noah entered his boat. 39 People didn't realize what was going to happen until the flood came and swept them all away. That is the way it will be when the Son of Man comes.

His point is that prior to the event he refers to, things will remain quite normal right up until the time of destruction. No one would see it coming, it would take them by surprise. Now read it again all together:

> 24:37 "When the Son of Man returns, it will be like it was in Noah's day. 38 In those days before the Flood, the people were enjoying banquets and parties and weddings right up to the time

Noah entered his boat. 39 People didn't realize what was going to happen until the flood came and swept them all away. That is the way it will be when the Son of Man comes. 40 "Two men will be working together in the field; one will be taken, the other left. 41 Two women will be grinding flour at the mill; one will be taken, the other left. 42 So be prepared, because you don't know what day your Lord is coming."

Now, remember the phrase, "I want to be left behind?" Consider this: in Jesus' analogy of Noah's day, who was taken, and who was left? We read: "People didn't realize what was going to happen until the flood came and swept them all away." The wicked people didn't see it coming, and were swept away by the flood. Noah and the other righteous people were saved, and left behind to re-inhabit the earth. In Jesus' example, the wicked are taken away, the righteous are left behind. Therefore the statement, "I want to be left behind" is equal to a call for being in righteousness according to Jesus' analogy, isn't it? Does this surprise you?

I ask you to consider this question: was Jesus speaking about a rapture, or a coming destruction of evil people akin to Noah's flood? Remember Matthew 23? When Jesus announced the "accumulated judgment of the centuries" would break on that generation, could he possibly be referring to that in Matthew 24? Just something to think about....

3

"This Generation Shall Not Pass Away…" or The Verse That Wouldn't Die!

What would you think if I told you there is one verse, one single verse upon which everyone's interpretation of biblical eschatology hinges? Would you believe that? If so, can you imagine what that verse is, or where to find it? If you're looking towards Matthew 24, you're right on. There is one single verse of scripture whose interpretation determines the entire effect of the rest of scripture. This is the other particular I spoke of in the last chapter: a particular detail so large and significant, everyone who wants to understand scripture, prophecy, and the world they live in has to understand the implications of such a detail. Remember I said this detail was open for debate within the church? This verse and its meaning has been debated by some pretty solid theologians on all sides of the debate. The question at hand is this: how does one examine this key verse, and determine its meaning? That is the essence of this chapter. No eschatological construct can ignore this verse, so neither should we. The LB story's validity hinges on the interpretation of this verse. So we are going to look at the verse and its various interpretations, and I will invite you to examine the evidence for yourself. Remember our goal: a critical examination of ideas to see if they come from Christ, or from the world. Let's get started….

By now you're probably ready to get to this unbelievably significant verse, right? The verse is Jesus' own words, a part of the Olivet Discourse. Look at the words of Matthew 24:34:

> 34 I assure you, this generation will not pass from the scene before all these things take place.

Do you feel as sense of letdown with this verse? Did you expect the verse would have Jesus speaking more words, or with more apocalyptic language? Sorry if it disappoints you, but this is the verse upon which all other prophecy and scripture hinges. Let me prove it to you:

From the time the disciples ask Jesus the question, to the time when he makes the statement in verse 34—about 30 verses have been spoken. These verses predict some very important and cataclysmic events. For example:

- False messiahs and false prophets would appear

- Wars and rumors of wars would break out

- Famines and earthquakes would take place all over the world

- God's people would be arrested, persecuted, and killed and hated all over the world

- Sin would be rampant everywhere

- The Gospel would be preached throughout the whole world so all nations would hear it

- The "abomination of desolation" spoken of in Daniel would take place

- A time of greater horror and tribulation than was ever seen before, or would ever be seen again

- The sun would be darkened, the moon would not give light, the stars would fall, and the heavens shaken

- The sign of the coming of the Son of Man would appear in the heavens

- The nations of the earth would see the Son of Man arrive on the clouds of heaven with power and glory

- The Son of Man would send forth his angels to gather his elect from the farthest ends of heaven

Wow. Lots of powerful stuff in that list!! Jesus listed and described these events as he said they would happen. Then right after describing these things, he says:

> 34 I assure you, this generation will not pass from the scene before all these things take place.

Huh? Let's get this straight: the disciples ask Jesus about the destruction of the temple and the coming judgment on the Jews, and he gives this great list of terrible things that will happen, ending in what appears to be some kind of "Rapture" type event. Then he caps it off with a statement like this:

> 34 I assure you, this generation will not pass from the scene before all these things take place.

Do you see why the interpretation of that verse becomes so critical? If one interprets that verse to mean Jesus is referring to the generation he was living in, the very same generation he had pronounced the ultimate judgment of the centuries upon, then clearly all these events either happened within 40 years of the discourse, or Jesus Christ's prophecy was wrong! If one interprets that the verse does not refer to the generation alive at the time of Jesus, one must explain the purpose

of Jesus' statement, and what he meant by it. I've heard some interesting interpretations. Not the least of which is the LB interpretation.
Let's look at it:

The LB position is pre-millennial, remember? They believe New
Testament prophecy is still unfulfilled. So they would certainly not
interpret verse 34 literally as the generation of people alive at that time.
Their interpretation is that the word translated "generation" can also
be translated to mean "race." This interpretation presumes the only
sound way to interpret this passage is like this:

> "I assure you, the nation of Israel will not pass from the scene
> before all these things take place."

This interpretation is interesting and has interesting logical out-
comes. It could be a valid interpretation, but does it come from Christ?
Is this interpretation the meaning Christ intended? The word in question here is the Greek word genea and appears many times in the New
Testament. In fact, if you remember our study of Matthew 23, when
Jesus announces "the accumulated judgment of the centuries" would
fall upon the people he was speaking to, he used the word genea. In
fact, there is not one example of the word genea being translated in
modern New Testament translations as a "race" or "nation," but rather
as the people who are alive at a particular time (an ancient exception:
the King James translation of Philippians 2:15, which, interestingly
enough, is translated as "generation" by the New King James, and a
leading premillennial scholar, John Darby). It is the word Jesus used
when he said, "A wicked and adulterous generation (genea) seeks a
miraculous sign, but none will be given it." If this word indeed means
that the Israelites, or the nation of Israel would not pass away until the
things happened, there is little or no previous use of that word in that
sense in scripture. I am not saying it can't be interpreted that way, or
even that is not what Jesus meant. I will ask the reader to study the
scriptures, analyze the other uses of that particular word in scripture,

and study the Greek context of the passage to find its meaning. Test this interpretation to see if it comes from Christ.

Let us assume for a moment this is the interpretation. If Jesus did mean:

> "I assure you, the race of Israel will not pass from the scene before all these things take place."

Would that make sense within the context of the passage? Remember the question at this point, for it holds part of the answer. If I told you the city you live in was going to be destroyed, and many of your friends and family were going to be killed in the process, you might ask me about this prophecy. If you believed me to be a prophet, your first question might be, "When will this happen?" If I then began to describe the signs of the times and the events leading up to the destruction of the city, and described the particulars surrounding the destruction, you would still be waiting for the punch line, right? Your question, after all, was when will this happen, right? If I finished my prophecy with this statement, would it make sense to you? Would it answer your question if I said:

I won't give you the exact date, but I assure you, the Anglo-Saxon race will not pass from the scene before this happens.

Or, on the other hand, would it answer you if I said:

I won't give you the exact date, but I assure you, the people who are alive right now will not pass from the scene before this happens.

Which answer best fits the question of "When will this destruction happen?" The first response fails to give you any useful information, doesn't it? The second one gives you a time-frame of the events to occur. Even if the argument can be made for the translation of the word genea into "race" or "nation," can it be made to sensibly answer the question of the disciples?

What if he meant the following definition:

I assure you, the people who are alive when all these things start to happen won't pass from the scene until all these things have taken place.

This is another popular interpretation that has given rise to strong feelings about the forming of the nation of Israel in 1948. Some people believe this indicates we are living in the end times because they believe the forming of Israel into a country is a sign. The LB folks believe that the 1948 generation won't pass until Christ comes (for the record, I do not believe there is any truth whatsoever to that theory, and I believe history will prove it wrong). While this "Zionist" theory seems possible, why would Jesus say all the things he said in Matthew 23, warn the disciples to be on their guard for troubling times and the destruction of the temple, and then make a statement regarding a society over 2000 years in the future? What in scripture makes us believe that Jesus would, without explanation, project his comments into the future over 20 centuries? Why would he not say to the disciples, "don't expect this to happen to you, it'll take place a long time from now." (Incidentally, Daniel was told some of his visions would be fulfilled a long time in the future, and he was not to expect them in his time) Jesus' discourse is full of warnings, spoken as if they would threaten the very people he was speaking to. Is there any reason whatsoever to project his comments into the future, rather than take them literally within context of Matthew 23?

If we interpret the statement to mean that everything listed in Matthew 24 prior to verse 34 would happen to the people in Jesus' day, does that seem unlikely? After all, there is a lot of terrible stuff there.

Could we possibly understand these things to have taken place already? Remember the list of things which were said to take place?

- False messiahs and false prophets would appear

- Wars and rumors of wars would break out

- Famines and earthquakes would take place all over the world

- God's people would be arrested, persecuted, and killed and hated all over the world

- Sin would be rampant everywhere

- The Gospel would be preached throughout the whole world so all nations would hear it

- The "abomination of desolation" spoken of in Daniel would take place

- A time of greater horror and tribulation than was ever seen before, or would ever be seen again

- The sun would be darkened, the moon would not give light, the stars would fall, and the heavens shaken

- The sign of the coming of the Son of Man would appear in the heavens

- The nations of the earth would see the Son of Man arrive on the clouds of heaven with power and glory

- The Son of Man would send forth his angels to gather his elect from the farthest ends of heaven

Either these things happened already, or they didn't. They are either fulfilled, or they are not. Either Jesus prophesied these things would take place in the day of the people he was with, or he did not. He cannot be referring to 2 different sets of events, for if he did, he would be contradicting himself. Can there be two of this event:

A time of greater horror and tribulation than was ever seen before, or would ever be seen again

No, of course not, there can not be two times of the worst trouble ever before or again, can there? Jesus was referring to one set of events in one period of time. One way or the other. One's interpretation of verse 34 becomes very important to the study, doesn't it? These events have either happened, or they have not. The way verse 34 is interpreted dictates our interpretation of the entire chapter, and virtually all of scripture. The consequences of the interpretation cannot be overstated.

Are you now trying to understand just how these events could have happened?

- False messiahs and false prophets would appear

- Wars and rumors of wars would break out

- Famines and earthquakes would take place all over the world

- God's people would be arrested, persecuted, and killed and hated all over the world

- Sin would be rampant everywhere

- The Gospel would be preached throughout the whole world so all nations would hear it

- The "abomination of desolation" spoken of in Daniel would take place

- A time of greater horror and tribulation than was ever seen before, or would ever be seen again

- The sun would be darkened, the moon would not give light, the stars would fall, and the heavens shaken

- The sign of the coming of the Son of Man would appear in the heavens

- The nations of the earth would see the Son of Man arrive on the clouds of heaven with power and glory

- The Son of Man would send forth his angels to gather his elect from the farthest ends of heaven

Could they have been fulfilled in Jesus' day? That is a good question, and we'll analyze that point in the next volume. This issue and the consequences surrounding the point are central to understanding LB doctrine and "end times" interpretation: is it possible that the events Jesus spoke of in Matthew 24 are already fulfilled, or must they be understood to still be future events? That is our next study. However, there is some "homework" for you to do. There is some Bible study you can do to prepare you for the next volume. Look at the following verses and answer the questions for each:

Acts chapter 2. What prophecy does Peter refer to from the Prophet Joel? Does Peter say that Joel's prophecy was fulfilled by what took place in Acts chapter 2? List each of the elements of Joel's prophecy, and then describe the events in Acts 2 that fulfilled each of the prophecies of Joel.

Daniel chapter 7. When Daniel refers to "the son of man," or "one who looked like a son of man," who is he referring to? When this "son of man" is seen coming on the clouds of heaven, where was he "coming" to? Where was he leaving from? Once he got to where he was "coming" to, what happened to him?

John chapter 11, verses 45-52. According to verse 52, what was the purpose of Jesus' death? What was significant about the High Priest's prophecy?

These studies will equip the reader to go to the next study. Try your very best to stay objective in your studies. Do not simply look up the meanings of these passages in a commentary, but meditate on the scriptures and their meanings. You'll be glad you did!

What do you think—is there one verse, one single verse upon which everyone's interpretation of biblical eschatology hinges? Do you believe that? There is one single verse of scripture whose interpretation determines the entire effect of the rest of scripture. This is the other particular I spoke of in the last chapter: a particular detail so large and significant, everyone who wants to understand scripture, prophecy, and the world they live in has to understand the implications of such a detail. Remember I said this detail was open for debate within the church? This verse and its meaning has been debated by some pretty solid theologians on all sides of the debate. No eschatological construct can ignore this verse, so neither should you. The LB story's validity hinges on the interpretation of this verse. I invite you to examine the evidence for yourself. Remember our goal: a critical examination of ideas to see if they come from Christ, or from the world.

Conclusion

The idea of reacting with noble character comes right from scripture. Study, refer, and check up on those who teach you. DO NOT believe anything anyone says just because they say it. The church should believe something because God has said it in His Word. The issue is not whether one adopts the "Left Behind" eschatology, the issue is the uncritical adoption of "Left Behind" or any other eschatology. My aim is to encourage the body to be like the Bereans. They adopted Paul's message based upon a careful consideration of his points. When the church studies eschatology, and adopts ideas and notions, it should be based on careful consideration of the teacher's points.

This book briefly outlined the major categories of eschatology interpretation, referred you to some books that go deeper into the issues, and scrutinize areas of the "Left Behind" theology to see if it really is the truth. In fact, much like the <u>Left Behind</u> series of books, this book is intended to be one of a series. The effort is to take the issues at hand in bite-sized portions, so as to keep things simple and understandable. The topic is controversial, sometimes difficult, and certainly not without complexities. The series will take things step-by-step in order to provide a clear approach to the purpose.

Keep in mind, the purpose of this series is not to persuade you to adopt or reject a particular doctrine. Colossians 2:8 says this: "Don't let anyone lead you astray with empty philosophy and high-sounding nonsense that come from human thinking and from the evil powers of this world, and not from Christ." (NLT) If any idea is true: it comes from Christ. If any idea is untrue, it comes from the world and human thinking. I am not out to get Tim LaHaye, or anybody else! I just want to encourage the body of Christ to adopt ideas that come from him based on critical analysis of His word. If that results in someone adopting the "Left Behind" ideas after critical examination, so be it! No bad feelings! The error comes from failure to examine the ideas against scripture to see if they are true. One day Christ will return! He'll demonstrate the truth for us Himself!

That loyalty to a doctrine or category of thought within the church is precisely what I invite the reader to check at the door as we begin this series. Our objectivity should be based on Colossians 2:8, and Acts 17:11, and other scriptures. Our ability to compare scripture with scripture to gain understanding is exactly what will help us in this analysis. Take a look at the books referred to you here, and examine the scriptures as you study. Also ask God to illuminate the scriptures as you study. The Holy Spirit will make the Word come alive to you. Without the Spirit, studying scripture is like reading someone else's mail: many meanings and points are lost.

One last thing I want to pass on to you: if you're just now reading about Jesus, or if the "Left Behind" books were your first exposure to Jesus, then I want you to think about something else. Jesus told people while He was on earth that they should repent of their sins, believe that He was the Son of God, and become students of his teachings and obey them. He explained to them that if they did not believe He was the Son of God, they would not be able to avoid going to Hell when they died. Their sins would keep them from going to be with God. The same goes for us today. If you have never thought about Jesus and whether He is God, please think about it. He is God's son, sent to pay the price for our sins, so we can be with Him in heaven. If you believe this, make sure you are obedient to what He told us to do, be baptized and become a student of His commands and obey them. Any studies of end times, or the apocalypse, or anything else pales in importance when it comes to this issue. Jesus asked, "what does it profit a man if he gains the whole world, and forfeits His soul?" I want you to gain understanding by studying this book, but I'd rather you not gain all understanding and forfeit your soul. Think about it: Jesus is the Son of

God, and he proved it when he was raised from the dead. That's a big deal—let's not forget about that in our studies! I'm thankful to Him for what He has done for us. I just want to point that out, and say, "Thanks" to Him. I hope you know Him, too!

Epilogue

A bold prediction was made that Jesus Christ was going to return in 1988. Soon after that failed prediction, I started my investigation into the claims Jesus made about himself, and was converted to Christianity. I became affiliated with a local church, and began attending Sunday school. Shortly after this time, my teachers introduced me to the pre-millennial view of eschatology. They taught about the rapture of the church, the antichrist and a 7-year tribulation. Not once was I ever led by these teachers to seriously study any other view of eschatology but the pre-millennial view. I studied this teaching for several years and truly believed this was how the world was going to end. As I grew up, and moved from church to church it became evident the pre-millennial view was the only view taught and accepted by all. A few years later the book, <u>Left Behind,</u> was published and I read it from cover to cover. This book was a novel supporting the pre-millennial view. I was a strong supporter of this book and recommended it to both Christians and non-Christians. However, in the spring of 2000, I was challenged to study the claims the Left behind series made in light of proper scriptural interpretation. When I was first confronted with the idea that maybe there was some error to the LB theory I was offended and outraged. How could I be so wrong? Isn't this the way the end of the world was supposed to play out? Weren't my bible teachers right about everything? After approximately 2 years of study, and many intense discussions, I have come to the conclusion that there are some improper biblical interpretations made in the very framework of the LB theory. If a person is willing to be objective and open to proper biblical interpretation, one can see these errors in the LB theory. I hope through this book, your thinking will be challenged, and you will search the scriptures, just as the Bereans did, to find out if what you have been taught is true. As one who used to stand solidly on the LB theory, I plead with you to test these claims and see if they come from Christ or from the world. May God bless you as you begin your study!

Brandon Jackson
Associate Pastor, Byron Fellowship Church

Appendix of Historical Citations

This section of this book is a work in progress. It is a collection of several notable quotations from several ancient historians. Origen, Josephus, Eusebius, and others documented historical facts about the time after Jesus' earthly ministry and about the early church. Why study this history? In order to understand scripture, one must understand the historical context of scripture, and the events that followed important Bible prophecy. We must understand the past in order to understand the future.

I will revise this collection in each successive volume of this series. It is not necessarily meant to be read as a chapter of this book, but rather a reference for further study on the topic of Bible history and eschatology. I hope it is helpful to you. I will note and comment on particular passages from historians that I find of significance. I will add to this body of work as further research dictates. Note that italics are my way of emphasizing a portion of the text, and boldface type represents my comments about the citations.

Have fun!

1. Josephus

Josephus was a Jewish historian who documented the history of the Jewish people from the early days of Israel to the time of Israel's destruction in 70 A.D. He was born in 37 A.D., and was an eyewitness to the Roman siege of Jerusalem, and the subsequent devastation of Israel in the Roman war. His vantage point on history is very interesting because he was able to work with the Roman leadership and document the events of his day without harm, though he was a Jew. Definitely some interesting insights on events that happened to the generation Jesus pronounced "all the accumulated judgment of the centuries" upon.

This first citation is a prelude to the events of the Roman invasion. There are several interesting points Josephus makes, but notice his recognition of impending doom on the Jews.

Book XX, Chapter VIII, Section 5

---

5. Now as for the affairs of the Jews, they grew worse and worse continually, for the country was again filled with robbers and impostors, who deluded the multitude. Yet did Felix catch and put to death many of those impostors every day, together with the robbers. He also caught Eleazar, the son of Dineas, who had gotten together a company of robbers; and this he did by treachery; for he gave him assurance that he should suffer no harm, and thereby persuaded him to come to him; but when he came, he bound him, and sent him to Rome. Felix also bore an ill-will to Jonathan, the high priest, because he frequently gave him admonitions about governing the Jewish affairs better than he did, lest he should himself have complaints made of him by the multitude, since he it was who had desired Caesar to send him as procurator of Judea. So Felix contrived a method whereby he might get rid of him, now he was become so continually troublesome to him; for such continual admonitions are grievous to those who are disposed to act unjustly. Wherefore Felix persuaded one of Jonathan's most faithful friends, a citizen of Jerusalem, whose name was Doras, to bring the robbers upon Jonathan, in order to kill him; and this he did by promising to give him a great deal of money for so doing. Doras complied with the proposal, and contrived matters so, that the robbers might murder him after the following manner: Certain of those robbers went up to the city, as if they were going to worship God, while they had

daggers under their garments, and by thus mingling themselves among the multitude they slew Jonathan and as this murder was never avenged, the robbers went up with the greatest security at the festivals after this time; and having weapons concealed in like manner as before, and mingling themselves among the multitude, they slew certain of their own enemies, and were subservient to other men for money; and slew others, not only in remote parts of the city, but in the temple itself also; for they had the boldness to murder men there, without thinking of the impiety of which they were guilty. *And this seems to me to have been the reason why God, out of his hatred of these men's wickedness, rejected our city; and as for the temple, he no longer esteemed it sufficiently pure for him to inhabit therein, but brought the Romans upon us, and threw a fire upon the city to purge it; and brought upon us, our wives, and children, slavery, as desirous to make us wiser by our calamities.*

Notice in the next section, he notes a false prophet, and the consequences.

Book XX, Chapter VIII, Section 6

---

6. These works, that were done by the robbers, filled the city with all sorts of impiety. And now these impostors and deceivers persuaded the multitude to follow them into the wilderness (1), and pretended that they would exhibit manifest wonders and signs, that should be performed by the providence of God. And many that were prevailed on by them suffered the punishments of their folly; for Felix brought them back, and then punished them. *Moreover, there came out of Egypt about this time to Jerusalem one that said he was a prophet, and advised the multitude of the common people to go along with him to the Mount of Olives, as it was called, which lay over against the city, and at the distance of five furlongs. He said further, that he would show them from hence how, at his command, the walls of Jerusalem would fall down; and he promised them that he would procure them an entrance into the city through those walls,*

when they were fallen down. Now when Felix was informed of these things, he ordered his soldiers to take their weapons, and came against them with a great number of horsemen and footmen from Jerusalem, and attacked the Egyptian and the people that were with him. He also slew four hundred of them, and took two hundred alive. But the Egyptian himself escaped out of the fight, but did not appear any more. And again the robbers stirred up the people to make war with the Romans, and said they ought not to obey them at all; and when any persons would not comply with them, they set fire to their villages, and plundered them.

Here, Josephus notes wars, rumors of wars, and his desire to be objective in relating the truth. He also calls the war the greatest ever heard of.

PREFACE, Section 1

1. *Whereas the war which the Jews made with the Romans hath been the greatest of all those, not only that have been in our times, but, in a manner, of those that were ever heard of; both of those wherein cities have fought against cities, or nations against nations;* while some men who were not concerned in the affair themselves, have gotten together vain and contradictory stories by heresay , and have written them down after a sophistical manner; and while those things that were then present have given false accounts of things, and this either out of a humour of flattery to the Romans, or of a hatred to the Jews; and while their writings contain sometimes accusations, and sometimes ecomiums, but nowhere the accurate truth of the facts, I have proposed to myself, for the sake of such as live under the government of the Romans, to translate those books into the Greek tongue, which I formerly composed in the language of our own country, and sent to the Upper Barbarians; I, Joseph, the son of Matthias, by birth a Hebrew, a priest also, and one who at first fought against the Romans myself, and was forced to be present at what was done afterwards....

Josephus claims the Jews got just what they asked for from the Romans. He obviously feels their evil was deserving of their destruction.

PREFACE, Section 4, Section 11

4. However, I will not go to the other extreme, out of opposition to those men who extol the Romans, nor will I determine to raise the actions of my countrymen too high; but I will prosecute the actions of both parties with accuracy. *Yet I shall suit my language to the passions I am under, as to the affairs I describe, and must be allowed to indulge some lamentation upon the miseries undergone by my own country; for that it was a seditious temper of our own that destroyed it; and that they were the tyrants among the Jews who brought the Roman power upon us, who unwillingly attacked us, and occasioned the burning of our holy temple; Titus Caesar, who destroyed it, is himself a witness, who, during the entire war, pitied the people who were kept under by the seditious, and did often voluntarily delay the taking of the city, and allowed time to the siege, in order to let the authors have opportunity for repentance.* But if anyone makes an unjust accusation against us, when we speak so passionately about the tyrants, or the robbers, or sorely bewail the misfortunes of our country, let him indulge our affections herein, though it be contrary to the rules for writing history; because it had so come to pass, that our city Jerusalem had arrived at a higher degree of felicity than any other city under the Roman government, and yet at last fell into the sorest calamities again. Accordingly it appears to me, that the misfortunes of all men, from the beginning of the world, if they be compared to these of the Jews, are not so considerable as they were; while the authors of them were not foreigners neither. This makes it impossible for me to contain my lamentations. But, if any one be inflexible in his censures of me, let him attribute the facts themselves to the historical part, and the lamentations to the writer himself only.

11. After this, I shall relate the barbarity of the tyrants toward the people of their own nation, as well as the indulgence of the Romans in sparing foreigners; and how often Titus, out of his desire to preserve the city and the temple, invited the seditious to come to terms of accommodation. I shall also distinguish the sufferings of the people, and their calamities; how far they were afflicted by the sedition, and how far, by the famine, and at length were taken. Nor shall I omit to mention the misfortunes of the deserters, nor the punishments inflicted on the captives; as also how the temple was burnt against the consent of Caesar; and how many sacred things that had been laid up in the temple, were snatched out of the fire; the destruction also of the entire city, with the signs and wonders that went before it; and the taking the tyrants captive, and the multitude of those that were made slaves, and into what different misfortunes they were every one distributed. Moreover, what the Romans did to the remains of the wall; and how they demolished the strongholds that were in the country; and how Titus went over the whole country, and settled its affairs; together with his return to Italy, and his triumph.

How it all began, according to Josephus....

Book II, Chapter XVII, Section 1, 2, 3, 4

How The War Of The Jews With The Romans Began

1. This advice the people hearkened to, and went up into the temple with the king and Bernice, and began to rebuild the cloisters: the rulers also and the senators divided themselves into the villages, and collected the tributes, and soon got together forty talents, which was the sum that was deficient. And thus did Agrippa then put a stop to that war which was threatened. Moreover, he attempted to persuade the multitude to obey Florus, until Caesar should send one to succeed him; but they were hereby more provoked, and cast reproaches upon the king, and got him excluded out of the city; nay, some of the seditious had

the imprudence to throw stones at him. So when the king saw that the violence of those that were for innovations was not be restrained, and being very angry at contumelies he had received, he sent their rulers, together with their men of power, to Florus, to Cesarea, that he might appoint whom he thought fit to collect the tribute in the country, while he retired into his own kingdom.

2. And at this time it was that some of those that principally excited the people to go to war, made an assault upon a certain fortress called Masada. They took it by treachery, and slew the Romans that were there, and put others of their own party to keep it. At the same time Eleazar, the son of Ananias the high priest, a very bold youth, who was at that time governor of the temple, persuaded those that officiated in the divine service to receive no gift or sacrifice for any foreigner. And this was the true beginning of our war with the Romans : for they rejected the sacrifice of Caesar on this account: and when many of the high priests and principal men besought them not to omit the sacrifice, which it was customary for them to offer for their princes, they would not be prevailed upon. These relied much upon their multitude, for the most flourishing part of the innovators assisted them; but they had the chief regard to Eleazar, the governor of the temple.

3. Hereupon the men of power got together, and confered with the high priests, as did also the principal of the Pharisees; and thinking all was at stake, and that their calamities were becoming incurable, took counsel what was to be done. Accordingly, they determined to try what they could do with the seditious by words, and assembled the people before the brazen gate, which was that gate of the inner temple which looked towards the sunrising. *And, in the first place, they shewed the great indignation they had at this attempt for a revolt, and for their bringing so great a war upon their country: after which they confuted their pretence as unjustifiable, and told them, that their forefathers had adorned their temple in great part with donations bestowed on them by foreigners, and had always received what had been presented to them from foreign*

nations; and that they had been so far from rejecting any person's sacrifice, (which would be the highest instance of impiety,) that they had themselves placed those donations about the temple which were still visible, and had remained there so long a time: that they did now irritate the Romans to take arms against them, and invited them to make war upon them, and brought up novel rules of strange divine worship, and determined to run the hazard of having their city condemned for impiety, while they would not allow any foreigners but Jews only, either to sacrifice or worship therein. And if such a law should ever be introduced in the case of a single person only, he would have indignation at it, as an instance of inhumanity determined against him; while they have no regard to the Romans or to Caesar, and forbade even their oblations to be received also; that however they cannot but fear, lest, by thus rejecting their sacrifices, they shall not be allowed to offer their own; and that this city will lose its principality, unless they grow wiser quickly, and restore the sacrifices as formerly; and indeed amend the injury before the report of it comes to the ears of those that have been injured.

4. And as they said these things, they produced those priests that were skilful in the customs of their country, who made the report, that all their forefathers had received the sacrifices from foreign nations.—But still not one of the innovators would hearken to what was said; nay, those that ministered about the temple would not attend their divine service, but were preparing matters for beginning the war. So the men of power, perceiving that the sedition was too hard for them to subdue, and that the danger which would arise from the Romans would come upon them first of all, endeavored to save themselves, and sent ambassadors; some to Florus, the chief of whom was Simon the son of Ananias; and others to Agrippa, among whom the most eminent was Saul, and Antipas, and Costobarus, who were of the king's kindred; and they desired of them both that they would come with an army to the city, and cut off the sedition before it should be too hard to be subdued. Now this terrible message was good news to Florus; and because his design was to have a war kindled, he gave the ambassadors no answer at

all. But Agrippa was equally solicitous for those that were revolting, and for those against whom the war was to be made, and was desirous to preserve the Jews for the Romans, and the temple and metropolis for the Jews; he was also sensible that it was not for his own advantage that the disturbances should proceed; so he sent three thousand horsemen to the assistance of the people out of Auranitis, and Batanea, and Trachonitis, and these under Darius, the master of his horse; and Phillip the son of Jacimus, the general of his army.

Really bad stuff was going on....

Book II, Chapter XVIII, Section 2

The Calamities and Slaughters That Came Upon The Jews

---

2. However, the Syrians were even (equal) with the Jews in the multitude of the men whom they slew; for they killed those whom they caught in the cities, and that not only out of the hatred they bare them, as formerly, but to prevent the danger under which they were from them; so that the disorders in all Syria were terrible, and every city was divided into two armies encamped one against another, and the preservation of the one party was in the destruction of the other; so the day-time was spent in shedding blood, and the night in fear,—which was of the two the more terrible; for when the Syrians thought they had ruined the Jews, they had the Judaisers in suspicion also; and as each side did not care to slay those whom they only suspected on the other, so did they greatly fear them when they were mingled with the other, as if they were certainly foreigners. Moreover, greediness of gain was a provocation to kill the opposite party even to such as had of old appeared very mild and gentle towards them; for they without fear plundered the effects of the slain, and carried of the spoil of those whom they slew to their own houses, as if they had been gained in a set battle; and he was esteemed a man of honour who got the greatest share, as having prevailed over the greater number of his enemies. *It*

was then common to see cities filled with dead bodies, still lying unburied, and those of old men, mixed with infants all dead and scattered about together; women also lay amongst them, without any covering for their nakedness: you might then see the whole province full of inexplicable calamities, while the dread of still more barbarous practices which were threatened, was everywhere greater that what had been already perpetrated.

One of the most interesting facts of the war is how the Roman General, Cestius, actually pulled back from Jerusalem. Remember, Jesus told his disciples when they saw Jerusalem surrounded by armies, they would know it was about to be destroyed, and they should flee to the mountains? (Luke 21:20-22) I always wondered how they could flee if the city was surrounded. This retreat seems to provide a perfect opportunity to escape the city…if a person knew what was coming. Keep in mind here, Josephus says that the seditious thought they had won and pursued the Romans. If someone in the city believed Jesus Christ, and knew about Matthew 24, Mark 13, or Luke 21, they would certainly have left the city. All other people would be in the city, "left behind."

Book II, Chapter XIX, Section 6,7

WHAT CESTIUS DID AGAINST THE JEWS; AND HOW, UPON HIS BESIEGING JERUSALEM, HE RETREATED FROM THE CITY WITHOUT ANY JUST OCCASION IN THE WORLD. AS ALSO WHAT SEVERE CALAMITIES HE UNDER WENT FROM THE JEWS IN HIS RETREAT.

---

6. And now it was that a horrible fear seized upon the seditious, insomuch that many of them ran out of the city, as though it were to be taken immediately; but the people upon this took courage, and where the wicked part of the city gave ground, thither did they come, in order to set open the gates, and to admit Cestius (1) as their benefactor, who, had he but continued the siege a little longer, had certainly taken the

city; but it was, I suppose, owing to the aversion God had already at the city and the sanctuary, that he was hindered from putting an end to the war that very day.

7. It then happened that Cestius was not conscious either how the besieged despaired of success, nor how courageous the people were for him; and so he recalled his soldiers from the place, and by despairing of any expectation of taking it, without having received any disgrace, he retired from the city, without any reason in the world. But when the robbers perceived this unexpected retreat of his, they resumed their courage, and ran after the hinder parts of his army, and destroyed a considerable number of both their horsemen and footmen; and now Cestius lay all night at the camp which was at Scopus; and as he went off farther next day, he thereby invited the enemy to follow him, who still fell upon the hindmost, and destroyed them; they also fell upon the flank on each side of the army, and threw darts upon them obliquely, nor durst those that were hindmost turn back upon those who wounded them behind, as imagining that the multitude of those that pursued them was immense; nor did they venture to drive away those that pressed upon them on each side, because they were heavy with their arms, and were afraid of breaking their ranks to pieces, and because they saw the Jews were light, and ready for making incursions upon them. And this was the reason why the Romans suffered greatly, without being able to revenge themselves upon their enemies; so they were galled all the way, and their ranks were put into disorder, and those that were thus put out of their ranks were slain; among whom were Priscus, the commander of the sixth legion, and Longinus, the tribune, and Emilius Secundus, the commander of a troop of horsemen. So it was not without difficulty that they got to Gabao, their former camp, and that not without the loss of a great part of their baggage. There it was that Cestius staid two days, and was in great distress to know what he should do in these circumstances; but when on the third day he saw a still much greater number of enemies, and all the parts round about him full of Jews, he understood that his delay was to his own detriment, and that if he staid any longer there, he should have still more enemies upon him.

Vespasian was the General who replaced Cestius, and would become Caesar. His son, Titus, was the General who would eventually destroy Israel. Read about just how bad it got, and think about the passages of scripture that talk about seas turning into blood, and about "Wormwood." (Revelation 8)

Book III, Chapter X, Section 9

A Description of the Country of Gennesareth

9. But now, when the vessels were gotten ready, Vespasian put upon ship-board as many of his forces as he thought sufficient to be too hard for those that were upon the lake, and set sail after them. Now these which were driven into the lake could neither fly to the land, where all was in their enemies' hand, and in war against them; nor could they fight upon the level by sea, for their ships were small and fitted only for piracy; they were too weak to fight with Vespasian's vessels, and the mariners that were in them were so few, that they were afraid to come near the Romans, who attacked them in great numbers. However, as they sailed round about the vessels, and sometimes as they came near them, they threw stones at the Romans when they were a good way off, or came closer and fought them; yet did they receive the greatest harm themselves in both cases. As for the stones they threw at the Romans, they only made a sound one after another, for they threw them against such as were in their armor, while the Roman darts could reach the Jews themselves; and when they ventured to come near the Romans, they became sufferers themselves before they could do any harm to the ether, and were drowned, they and their ships together. As for those that endeavored to come to an actual fight, the Romans ran many of them through with their long poles. Sometimes the Romans leaped into their ships, with swords in their hands, and slew them; but when

some of them met the vessels, the Romans caught them by the middle, and destroyed at once their ships and themselves who were taken in them. And for such as were drowning in the sea, if they lifted their heads up above the water, they were either killed by darts, or caught by the vessels; but if, in the desperate case they were in, they attempted to swim to their enemies, *the Romans cut off either their heads or their hands; and indeed they were destroyed after various manners every where, till the rest being put to flight, were forced to get upon the land, while the vessels encompassed them about: but as many of these were repulsed when they were getting ashore, they were killed by the darts upon the lake; and the Romans leaped out of their vessels, and destroyed a great many more upon the land: one might then see the lake all bloody, and full of dead bodies, for not one of them escaped. And a terrible stink, and a very sad sight there was on the following days over that country; for as for the shores, they were full of shipwrecks, and of dead bodies all swelled; and as the dead bodies were inflamed by the sun, and putrefied, they corrupted the air, insomuch that the misery was not only the object of commiseration to the Jews, but to those that hated them, and had been the authors of that misery.*

Note in the following passage the occurrence of an earthquake-like storm which Josephus understood to portend the destruction of Jerusalem.

Book IV, Chapter IV, Section 5

Manifest Indications of Coming Destruction

---

5. And now did the Idumeans make an acclamation to what Simon had said; but Jesus [Not THE Jesus, but a priest named Jesus—tk] went away sorrowful, as seeing that the Idumeans were against all moderate counsels, and that the city was besieged on both sides. Nor indeed were the minds of the Idumeans at rest; for they were in a rage at the injury that had been offered them by their exclusion out of the city;

and when they thought the zealots had been strong, but saw nothing of theirs to support them, they were in doubt about the matter, and many of them repented that they had come thither. *But the shame that would attend them in case they returned without doing any thing at all, so far overcame that their repentance, that they lay all night before the wall, though in a very bad encampment; for there broke out a prodigious storm in the night, with the utmost violence, and very strong winds, with the largest showers of rain, with continued lightnings, terrible thunderings, and amazing concussions and bellowings of the earth, that was in an earth-quake. These things were a manifest indication that some destruction was coming upon men, when the system of the world was put into this disorder; and any one would guess that these wonders foreshowed some grand calamities that were coming.*

In this next passage, I am reminded of Jesus' description of a time of great tribulation in Matthew 24. Also, think about verses of scripture that speak about men longing for death (i.e. Revelation 6), then read this. Keep in mind, it gets worse....

Book IV, Chapter VI, Section 3

The Wickedness and Perversions of the Seditious Jews.

3. And now the commanders joined in their approbation of what Vespasian had said, and it was soon discovered how wise an opinion he had given. And indeed many there were of the Jews that deserted every day, and fled away from the zealots, although their flight was very difficult, since they had guarded every passage out of the city, and slew every one that was caught at them, as taking it for granted they were going over to the Romans; yet did he who gave them money get clear off, while he only that gave them none was voted a traitor. So the upshot was this, that the rich purchased their flight by money, while none but the poor were slain. Along all the roads also vast numbers of dead bodies lay in heaps, and even many of those that were so zealous

in deserting at length chose rather to perish within the city; for the hopes of burial made death in their own city appear of the two less terrible to them. But these zealots came at last to that degree of barbarity, as not to bestow a burial either on those slain in the city, or on those that lay along the roads; *but as if they had made an agreement to cancel both the laws of their country and the laws of nature, and, at the same time that they defiled men with their wicked actions, they would pollute the Divinity itself also, they left the dead bodies to putrefy under the sun; and the same punishment was allotted to such as buried any as to those that deserted, which was no other than death; while he that granted the favor of a grave to another would presently stand in need of a grave himself. To say all in a word, no other gentle passion was so entirely lost among them as mercy; for what were the greatest objects of pity did most of all irritate these wretches, and they transferred their rage from the living to those that had been slain, and from the dead to the living. Nay, the terror was so very great, that he who survived called them that were first dead happy, as being at rest already; as did those that were under torture in the prisons, declare, that, upon this comparison, those that lay unburied were the happiest. These men, therefore, trampled upon all the laws of men, and laughed at the laws of God; and for the oracles of the prophets, they ridiculed them as the tricks of jugglers; yet did these prophets foretell many things concerning virtue, and vice, which when these zealots violated, they occasioned the fulfilling of those very prophecies belonging to their own country; for there was a certain ancient oracle of those men, that the city should then be taken and the sanctuary burnt, by right of war, when a sedition should invade the Jews, and their own hand should pollute the temple of God. Now while these zealots did not disbelieve these predictions, they made themselves the instruments of their accomplishment.*

This next passage also reminds me of biblical descriptions of prophetic events. Think about the notion of the Jordan river being impassable due to the high number of dead bodies. Think about the Dead Sea, and its size, then read on.

Book IV, Chapter VII, Section 6

Account Of The Lake Asphaltitis (The Dead Sea)

---

6. Now, this destruction that fell upon the Jews, as it was not inferior to any of the rest in itself, so did it still appear greater than it really was; *and this, because not only the whole of the country through which they had fled was filled with slaughter, and Jordan could not be passed over, by reason of the dead bodies that were in it, but because the Lake Asphaltitis (The Dead Sea) was also full of dead bodies, that were carried down into it by the river.* And now, Placidus, after this good success that he had, fell violently upon the neighbouring smaller cities and villages; when he took Abila, and Julias, and Bezemoth, and all those that lay as far as the lake Asphaltitis, and put such of the deserters into each of them as he though proper. He then put his soldiers on board the ships, and slew such as had fled to the lake, insomuch that all Perea had either surrendered themselves, or were taken by the Romans, as far as Macherus.

Yes, this next passage really does include cross-dressing. I didn't make it up, either. Read on.

Book IV, Chapter IX, Section 10

The Pollutions of the Transvestite Leaders

---

10. And now, as soon as Simon had set his wife free, and recovered her from the zealots, he returned back to the remainders of Idumea, and driving the nation all before him from all quarters, he compelled a great number of them to retire to Jerusalem; he followed them himself also to the city, and encompassed the wall all round again; and when he lighted upon any laborers that were coming thither out of the country, he slew them. Now this Simon, who was without the wall, was a greater terror to the people than the Romans themselves, as were the zealots who were within it more heavy upon them than both of the

other; and during this time did the mischievous contrivances and courage corrupt the body of the Galileans; for these Galileans had advanced this John, and made him very potent, who made them suitable requital from the authority he had obtained by their means; *for he permitted them to do all things that any of them desired to do, while their inclination to plunder was insatiable, as was their zeal in searching the houses of the rich; and for the murdering of the men, and abusing of the women, it was sport to them. They also devoured what spoils they had taken, together with their blood, and indulged themselves in feminine wantonness, without any disturbance, till they were satiated therewith; while they decked their hair, and put on women's garments, and were besmeared over with ointments; and that they might appear very comely, they had paints under their eyes, and imitated not only the ornaments, but also the lusts of women, and were guilty of such intolerable uncleanness, that they invented unlawful pleasures of that sort. And thus did they roll themselves up and down the city, as in a brothel-house, and defiled it entirely with their impure actions; nay, while their faces looked like the faces of women, they killed with their right hands; and when their gait was effeminate, they presently attacked men, and became warriors, and drew their swords from under their finely dyed cloaks, and ran every body through whom they alighted upon.* However, Simon waited for such as ran away from John, and was the more bloody of the two; and he who had escaped the tyrant within the wall was destroyed by the other that lay before the gates, so that all attempts of flying and deserting to the Romans were cut off, as to those that had a mind so to do.

This next passage notes the unthinkable death and destruction within the city. Again, remember Jesus' words from Matthew 23 about the accumulated judgment of the centuries.

Book V, Chapter I, Section 3

What Terrible Miseries Afflicted the City

3. But now the tyrant Simon, the son of Gioras, whom the people had invited in, out of the hopes they had of his assistance in the great distresses they were in, having in his power the upper city, and a great part of the lower, did now make more vehement assaults upon John and his party, because they were fought against from above also; yet was he beneath their situation when he attacked them, as they were beneath the attacks of the others above them. Whereby it came to pass that John did both receive and inflict great damage, and that easily, as he was fought against on both sides; and the same advantage that Eleazar and his party had over him, since he was beneath them, the same advantage had he, by his higher situation, over Simon. *On which account he easily repelled the attacks that were made from beneath, by the weapons thrown from their hands only; but was obliged to repel those that threw their darts from the temple above him, by his engines of war; for he had such engines as threw darts, and javelins, and stones, and that in no small number, by which he did not only defend himself from such as fought against him, but slew moreover many of the priests, as they were about their sacred ministrations. For notwithstanding these men were mad with all sorts of impiety, yet did they still admit those that desired to offer their sacrifices, although they took care to search the people of their own country beforehand, and both suspected and watched them; while they were not so much afraid of strangers, who, although they had gotten leave of them, how cruel soever they were, to come into that court, were yet often destroyed by this sedition; for those darts that were thrown by the engines came with that force, that they went over all the buildings, and reached as far as the altar, and the temple itself, and fell upon the priests, and those that were about the sacred offices; insomuch that many persons who came thither with great zeal from the ends of the earth, to offer sacrifices at this celebrated place, which was esteemed holy by all mankind, fell down before their own sacrifices themselves, and sprinkled that altar which was venerable among all men, both Greeks and Barbarians, with their own blood; till the dead bodies of strangers were mingled together with those of their own country, and those of profane persons with those of the priests, and the*

blood of all sorts of dead carcasses stood in lakes in the holy courts themselves. And now, "O must wretched city, what misery so great as this didst thou suffer from the Romans, when they came to purify thee from thy intestine hatred! 'For thou couldst be no longer a place fit for God, nor couldst thou long continue in being, after thou hadst been a sepulcher for the bodies of thy own people, and hadst made the holy house itself a burying-place in this civil war of thine. Yet mayst thou again grow better, if perchance thou wilt hereafter appease the anger of that God who is the author of thy destruction." But I must restrain myself from these passions by the rules of history, since this is not a proper time for domestical lamentations, but for historical narrations; I therefore return to the operations that follow in this sedition.

We've already read of a false prophet that came on the scene, but there were 3 major leaders of factions within the city. This passage describes how these factions fought each other and the Romans. They also ended up cutting off their own food supply.

Book V, Chapter I, Section 4

The Destruction Of A Vast Quantity Of Corn
That Led To Famine During The Siege

4. And now there were three treacherous factions in the city, the one parted from the other. Eleazar and his party, that kept the sacred first-fruits, came against John in their cups. Those that were with John plundered the populace, and went out with zeal against Simon. This Simon had his supply of provisions from the city, in opposition to the seditious. When, therefore, John was assaulted on both sides, he made his men turn about, throwing his darts upon those citizens that came up against him, from the cloisters he had in his possession, while he opposed those that attacked him from the temple by engines of war; and if at any time he was freed from those that were above him, which happened frequently, from their being drunk and tired, he sallied out

with a great number upon Simon and his party; and this he did always in such parts of the city as he could come at, till he set on fire those houses that were full of corn, and of all provisions. The same thing was done by Simon, when, upon the others' retreat, he attacked the city also; as if they had, on purpose done it to serve the Romans, by destroying what the city had laid up against the Siege, and by thus cutting off the nerves of their own power. Accordingly, it so came to pass, that all the places that were about the temple were burnt down, and were become an intermediate desert space, ready for fighting on both sides; and that almost all the corn was burnt, which would have been sufficient for a siege of many years. So they were taken by the means of famine, which it was impossible they should have been, unless they had thus prepared the way for it by this procedure.

In this next passage, we see General Titus come on the scene, along with the rest of the Roman forces in the area. No one knew just how devastating the Romans could be.

Book V, Chapter I, Section 6

The Makeup of the Roman Army That Came Against Jerusalem

6. Thus did John hope to be too hard for his enemies by these engines constructed by his impiety; but God himself demonstrated that his pains would prove of no use to him, by bringing the Romans upon him, before he had reared any of his towers; for Titus, when he had gotten together part of his forces about him, and had ordered the rest to meet him at Jerusalem, marched out of Cesarea. He had with him those three legions that had accompanied his father when he laid Judea waste, together with that twelfth legion which had been formerly beaten with Cestius; which legion, as it was otherwise remarkable for its valor, so did it march on now with greater alacrity to avenge themselves on the Jews, as remembering what they had formerly suffered from them. Of these legions he ordered the fifth to meet him, by going

through Emmaus, and the tenth to go up by Jericho; he also moved himself, together with the rest; besides whom, marched those auxiliaries that came from the kings, being now more in number than before, together with a considerable number that came to his assistance from Syria. Those also that had been selected out of these four legions, and sent with Mucianus to Italy, had their places filled up out of these soldiers that came out of Egypt with Titus; who were two thousand men, chosen out of the armies at Alexandria. There followed him also three thousand drawn from those that guarded the river Euphrates; as also there came Tiberius Alexander, who was a friend of his, most valuable, both for his good-will to him, and for his prudence. He had formerly been governor of Alexandria, but was now thought worthy to be general of the army. The reason of this was, that he had been the first who encouraged Vespasian very lately to accept this his new dominion, and joined himself to him with great fidelity, when things were uncertain, and fortune had not yet declared for him. He also followed Titus as a counselor, very useful to him in this war, both by his age and skill in such affairs.

In this next passage, we read about Titus' "ensigns." These are the long standards with flags which bear the sign of Rome: SPQR (Senatus Populus Que Romanus-The Senate and People of Rome). Next to the sign of Rome is a visage of Caesar, and the sign of the General who commands the army. In this case, the sign of Titus was an eagle. Just a tidbit of history, but it is very interesting to recall Jesus' words in Matthew 24: "For wheresoever the carcass is, there will the eagles be gathered together." Again in Luke 17:37 He says, "And they answered and said unto him, Where, Lord? And he said unto them, Wheresoever the body is, thither will the eagles be gathered together."

Now, I know many translations translate these verses with the word "vulture." However, the Greek word is literally, eagle. If you research the word, Aetos, in the <u>Thayer's and Smith's Bible Dictio-</u>

nary, (which is a great public domain resource available on the web) you will find it says:

1. **an eagle: since eagles do not usually go in quest of carrion, this may [sic] to a vulture that resembles an eagle**

2. **an eagle as a standard (Roman Military)**

Just something to think about...

Book V, Chapter II, Section 1

How Titus Marched To Jerusalem, and How He Was in Danger as he Was Taking a View of the City of the Place Also Where He Pitched His Camp

---

1. NOW, as Titus was upon his march into the enemy's country, the auxiliaries that were sent by the kings marched first, having all the other auxiliaries with them; after whom followed those that were to prepare the roads and measure out the camp; then came the commander's baggage, and after that the other soldiers, who were completely armed to support them; then came Titus himself, having with him another select body; and then came the pikemen; after whom came the horse belonging to that legion. *All these came before the engines; and after these engines came the tribunes and the leaders of the cohorts, with their select bodies; after these came the ensigns, with the eagle;* and before those ensigns came the trumpeters belonging to them; next these came the main body of the army in their ranks, every rank being six deep; the servants belonging to every legion came after these; and before these last their baggage; the mercenaries came last, and those that guarded them brought up the rear. Now Titus, according to the Roman usage, went in the front of the army after a decent manner, and marched through Samaria to Gophna, a city that had been formerly taken by his father, and was then garrisoned by Roman soldiers; and when he had lodged there one night, he marched on in the morning; and when he had gone as far as a day's march, he pitched his camp at that valley which the Jews, in their own tongue, call "the Valley of

Thorns," near a certain village called Gabaothsath, which signifies "the Hill of Saul," being distant from Jerusalem about thirty furlongs. There it was that he chose out six hundred select horsemen, and went to take a view of the city, to observe what strength it was of, and how courageous the Jews were; whether, when they saw him, and before they came to a direct battle, they would be affrighted and submit; for he had been informed what was really true, that the people who were fallen under the power of the seditious and the robbers were greatly desirous of peace; but being too weak to rise up against the rest, they lay still.

Notice in this next section how Titus is referred to as Caesar, and how his army encamped on the Mount of Olives. It is very interesting to note that the judgment of the Jews and Jerusalem came at the hands of an army encamped on the very same site where Jesus Christ foretold of its destruction.

Book V, Chapter II, Section 2

How Titus Marched To Jerusalem, and How He Was in Danger as he Was Taking a View of the City of the Place Also Where He Pitched His Camp

2. Now, so long as he rode along the straight road which led to the wall of the city, nobody appeared out of the gates; but when he went out of that road, and declined towards the tower Psephinus, and led the band of horsemen obliquely, an immense number of the Jews leaped out suddenly at the towers called the "Women's Towers," through that gate which was over against the monuments of queen Helena, and intercepted his horse; and standing directly opposite to those that still ran along the road, hindered them from joining those that had declined out of it. They intercepted Titus also, with a few other. Now it was here impossible for him to go forward, because all the places had trenches dug in them from the wall, to preserve the gardens round about, and were full of gardens obliquely situated, and of many hedges;

and to return back to his own men, he saw it was also impossible, by reason of the multitude of the enemies that lay between them; many of whom did not so much as know that the king was in any danger, but supposed him still among them. So he perceived that his preservation must be wholly owing to his own courage, and turned his horse about, and cried out aloud to those that were about him to follow him, and ran with violence into the midst of his enemies, in order to force his way through them to his own men. And hence we may principally learn, that both the success of wars, and the dangers that kings are in, are under the providence of God; for while such a number of darts were thrown at Titus, when he had neither his head-piece on, nor his breastplate, (for, as I told you, he went out not to fight, but to view the city,) none of them touched his body, but went aside without hurting him; as if all of them missed him on purpose, and only made a noise as they passed by him. So he diverted those perpetually with his sword that came on his side, and overturned many of those that directly met him, and made his horse ride over those that were overthrown. *The enemy indeed made a shout at the boldness of Caesar, and exhorted one another to rush upon him. Yet did these against whom he marched fly away, and go off from him in great numbers; while those that were in the same danger with him kept up close to him, though they were wounded both on their backs and on their sides; for they had each of them but this one hope of escaping, if they could assist Titus in opening himself a way, that he might not be encompassed round by his enemies before he got away from them.* Now there were two of those that were with him, but at some distance; the one of which the enemy compassed round, and slew him with their darts, and his horse also; but the other they slew as he leaped down from his horse, and carried off his horse with them. But Titus escaped with the rest, and came safe to the camp. So this success of the Jews' first attack raised their minds, and gave them an ill-grounded hope; and this short inclination of fortune, on their side, made them very courageous for the future.

Book V, Chapter II, Section 3

How Titus Marched To Jerusalem, and How He Was in Danger as he Was Taking a View of the City of the Place Also Where He Pitched His Camp

---

3. But now, as soon as that legion that had been at Emmaus was joined to Caesar at night, he removed thence, when it was day, and came to a place called Seopus; from whence the city began already to be seen, and a plain view might be taken of the great temple. Accordingly, this place, on the north quarter of the city, and joining thereto, was a plain, and very properly named Scopus, [the prospect,] and was no more than seven furlongs distant from it. And here it was that Titus ordered a camp to be fortified for two legions that were to be together; but ordered another camp to be fortified, at three furlongs farther distance behind them, for the fifth legion; for he thought that, by marching in the night, they might be tired, and might deserve to be covered from the enemy, and with less fear might fortify themselves; and as these were now beginning to build, the tenth legion, who came through Jericho, was already come to the place, where a certain party of armed men had formerly lain, to guard that pass into the city, and had been taken before by Vespasian. *These legions had orders to encamp at the distance of six furlongs from Jerusalem, at the mount called the Mount of Olives which lies over against the city on the east side, and is parted from it by a deep valley, interposed between them, which is named Cedron.*

This next passage identifies the leadership of the revolt within Jerusalem, and the numbers of the parties. Note, too, that Josephus remarks that the sedition (revolt) destroyed the city, and the Romans destroyed the sedition. I find it interesting that God's judgment included death at their own hands within Jerusalem.

Book V, Chapter III, Section 1

How The Sedition was Again Revived Within Jerusalem and yet the Jews Contrived Snares for the Romans

---

1. Now the warlike men that were in the city, and the multitude of the seditious that were with Simon, were ten thousand, besides the Idumeans. Those ten thousand had fifty commanders, over whom this Simon was supreme. The Idumeans that paid him homage were five thousand, and had eight commanders, among whom those of the greatest fame were Jacob, the son of Sosas, and Simon, the son of Cathlas. John, who had seized upon the temple, had six thousand armed men, under twenty commanders; the zealots also that had come over to him, and left off their opposition, were two thousand four hundred, and had the same commander they had formerly, Eleazar, together with Simon, the son of Arinus. Now, while these factions fought one against another, the people were their prey of both sides, as we have said already; and that part of the people who would not join with them in their wicked practices, were plundered by both factions. Simon held the upper city, and the great walls as far as Cedron, and as much of the old wall as bent from Siloam to the east, and which went down to the palace of Monobazus, who was king of the Adiabeni, beyond Euphrates; he also held the fountain, and the Acra, which was no other than the lower city; he also held all that reached to the palace of queen Helena, the mother of Monobazus; but John held the temple, and the parts thereto adjoining, for a great way, as also Ophla, and the valley called "Valley of Cedron;" and when the parts that were interposed between their possessions were burnt by them, they left a space wherein they might fight with each other; for this internal sedition did not cease, even when the Romans were encamped near their very walls. But although they had grown wiser at the first onset the Romans made upon them, this lasted but for a while; for they returned to their former madness, and separated one from another, and fought it out, and did everything that the besiegers could desire them to do; for they never

suffered anything that was worse from the Romans than they made each other suffer; nor was there any misery endured by the city after these men's actions that could be esteemed new. But it was most of all unhappy before it was overthrown, while those that took it did it a greater kindness; for I venture to affirm, that the sedition destroyed the city, and the Romans destroyed the sedition, which it was a much harder thing to do that to destroy the walls; so that we may justly ascribe our misfortunes to our own people, and the just vengeance taken on them by the Romans; as to which matter let every one determine by the actions on both sides.

In this next section, keep in mind Revelation chapter 16, remember the divisions within the city, Jesus' prophecy of the accumulated judgment of the centuries, and the events which preceded this event. Then read on...

Rev 16:18 "Then the thunder crashed and rolled, and lightning flashed. And there was an earthquake greater than ever before in human history. 19 The great city of Babylon split into three pieces, and cities around the world fell into heaps of rubble. And so God remembered all of Babylon's sins, and he made her drink the cup that was filled with the wine of his fierce wrath. 20 And every island disappeared, and all the mountains were leveled. 21 There was a terrible hailstorm, and hailstones weighing seventy-five pounds [Greek: one talent] fell from the sky onto the people below. They cursed God because of the hailstorm, which was a very terrible plague."

Book V, Chapter VI, Section 3

Hailstones One Hundred Pounds in Weight Thrown Upon City

---

3. However, John stayed behind, out of his fear of Simon, even while his own men were earnest in making a sally upon their enemies with-

out. Yet did not Simon lie still, for he lay near the place of the siege; he brought his engines of war, and disposed of them at due distances upon the wall, both those which they took from Cestius formerly, and those which they got when they seized the garrison that lay in the tower Antonia. But though they had these engines in their possession, they had so little skill in using them, that they were in great measure useless to them; but a few there were who had been taught by deserters how to use them, which they did use, though after an awkward manner. So they cast stones and arrows at those that were making the banks; they also ran out upon them by companies, and fought with them. Now those that were at work covered themselves with hurdles spread over their banks, and their engines were opposed to them when they made their excursions. The engines, that all the legions had ready prepared for them, were admirably contrived; but still more extraordinary ones belonged to the tenth legion: those that threw darts and those that threw stones were more forcible and larger than the rest, by which they not only repelled the excursions of the Jews, but drove those away that were upon the walls also. *Now the stones that were cast were of the weight of a talent, and were carried two furlongs and further. The blow they gave was no way to be sustained, not only by those that stood first in the way, but by those that were beyond them for a great space. As for the Jews, they at first watched the coming of the stone, for it was of a white color, and could therefore not only be perceived by the great noise it made, but could be seen also before it came by its brightness; accordingly the watchmen that sat upon the towers gave them notice when the engine was let go, and the stone came from it, and cried out aloud, in their own country language, THE STONE COMETH so those that were in its way stood off, and threw themselves down upon the ground; by which means, and by their thus guarding themselves, the stone fell down and did them no harm. But the Romans contrived how to prevent that by blacking the stone, who then could aim at them with success, when the stone was not discerned beforehand, as it had been till then; and so they destroyed many of them at one blow.* Yet did not the Jews, under all this distress, permit the

Romans to raise their banks in quiet; but they shrewdly and boldly exerted themselves, and repelled them both by night and by day.

This next section documents Josephus' plea to the Jews that they repent and give up. Notice he reasons with history, and with a moral appeal based on their behavior. He also says they are as dumb as rocks. Obviously, they reject him.

Book V, Chapter IX, Section 4 (Partial)

Josephus Sent By Titus To Discourse With Countrymen

4. While Josephus was making this exhortation to the Jews, many of them jested upon him from the wall, and many reproached him; nay, some threw their darts at him: but when he could not himself persuade them by such open good advice, he betook himself to the histories belonging to their own nation, and cried out aloud, O miserable creatures! are you so unmindful of those that used to assist you, that you will fight by your weapons and by your hands against the Romans? When did we ever conquer any other nation by such means? and when was it that God, who is the Creator of the Jewish people, did not avenge them when they had been injured? Will not you turn again, and look back, and consider whence it is that you fight with such violence, and how great a Supporter you have profanely abused? Will not you recall to mind the prodigious things done for your forefathers and this holy place, and how great enemies of yours were by him subdued under you? I even tremble myself in declaring the works of God before your ears, that are unworthy to hear them; however, hearken to me, that you may be informed how you fight not only against the Romans, but against God himself. In old times there was one Necao, king of Egypt, who was also called Pharaoh; he came with a prodigious army of soldiers, and seized queen Sarah, the mother of our nation. What did Abraham our progenitor then do? Did he defend himself from this injurious person by war, although he had three hundred and eighteen

captains under him, and an immense army under each of them? Indeed he deemed them to be no number at all without God's assistance, and only spread out his hands towards this holy place, which you have now polluted, and reckoned upon him as upon his invincible supporter, instead of his own army. Was not our queen sent back, without any defilement, to her husband, the very next evening?—while the king of Egypt fled away, adoring this place which you have defiled by shedding thereon the blood of your own countrymen; and he also trembled at those visions which he saw in the night season, and bestowed both silver and gold on the Hebrews, as on a people beloved by God. Shall I say nothing, or shall I mention the removal of our fathers into Egypt, who, when they were used tyrannically, and were fallen under the power of foreign kings for four hundred ears together, and might have defended themselves by war and by fighting, did yet do nothing but commit themselves to God! Who is there that does not know that Egypt was overrun with all sorts of wild beasts, and consumed by all sorts of distempers? how their land did not bring forth its fruit? how the Nile failed of water? how the ten plagues of Egypt followed one upon another? and how by those means our fathers were sent away under a guard, without any bloodshed, and without running any dangers, because God conducted them as his peculiar servants? ..It was God who then became our General, and accomplished these great things for our fathers, and this because they did not meddle with war and fighting, but committed it to him to judge about their affairs. ...And, to speak in general, we can produce no example wherein our fathers got any success by war, or failed of success when without war they committed themselves to God. When they stayed at home, they conquered, as pleased their Judge; but when they went out to fight, they were always disappointed: for example, when the king of Babylon besieged this very city, and our king Zedekiah fought against him, contrary to what predictions were made to him by Jeremiah the prophet, he was at once taken prisoner, and saw the city and the temple demolished. Yet how much greater was the moderation of that king, than is that of your present governors, and that of the people then under him, than is that of you at this time! for when Jeremiah cried out aloud, how very angry God was at them, because of their transgressions, and told them they should be taken prisoners, unless they would surrender up their city, neither did the king nor the people put him to death; but for you, (to pass over what you have done within the city, which I am not able to describe as your wickedness deserves,) you abuse me, and throw darts at me, who only exhort you to save yourselves, as being provoked when you are put in mind of your sins, and cannot bear the very mention of those crimes which you every day perpetrate. For another example, when Antiochus, who was called Epiphanes, lay before this city, and had been guilty of many indignities against God, and our forefathers met him in arms, they then were slain in the battle, this city was plundered by our enemies, and our sanctuary made desolate for three years and six months. And what need I bring any more examples? Thus it appears that arms were never given to our nation, but that we are always given up to be fought against, and to be taken; for I suppose that such as inhabit this holy place ought to commit the disposal of all things to God, and then only to disregard the assistance of men when they resign themselves up to their Arbitrator, who is above. As for you, what have you done of those things that are recommended by our legislator? and what have you not done of those things that he hath condemned? How much more impious are you than those who were so quickly taken! You have not avoided so much as those sins that are usually done in secret; I mean thefts, and treacherous plots against men, and adulteries. You are quarrelling about rapines and murders, and invent strange ways of wickedness. Nay, the temple itself is become the receptacle of all, and this Divine place is polluted by the hands of those of our own country; which place hath yet been reverenced by the Romans when it was at a distance from them, when they have suffered many of their own customs to give place to our law. And, after all this, do you expect Him whom you have so impiously abused to be your supporter? To be sure then you have a right to be petitioners, and to call upon Him to assist you, so pure are your hands! And it is plain madness to expect that God should appear as well disposed towards the wicked as towards the righteous, since he knows when it is proper to punish men for their sins immediately; accordingly he brake the power of the Assyrians the very first night that they pitched their camp. Wherefore, had he judged that our nation was worthy of freedom, or the Romans of punishment, he had immediately inflicted punishment upon those Romans, as he did upon the Assyrians, when Pompey began to meddle with our nation, or when after him Sosius came up against us, or when Vespasian laid waste Galilee, or, lastly, when Titus came first of all near to this city; although Magnus and Sosius did not only suffer nothing, but took the city by force; as did Vespasian go from the war he made against you to receive the empire; and as for Titus, those springs that were formerly almost dried up when they were under your power since he is come, run more plentifully than they did before; accordingly, you know that Siloam, as well as all the other springs that were without the city, did so far fail, that water was sold by distinct measures; whereas they now have such a great quantity of water for your enemies, as is sufficient not only for drink both for themselves and their cattle, but for watering their gardens also. The same wonderful sign you had also experience of formerly, when the forementioned king of Babylon made war against us, and when he took the city, and burnt the temple; while yet I believe the Jews of that age were not so impious as you are. Wherefore I cannot but suppose that God is fled out of his sanctuary, and stands on the side of those against whom you fight

Now even a man, if he be but a good man, will fly from an impure house, and will hate those that are in it; and do you persuade yourselves that God will abide with you in your iniquities, who sees all secret things, and hears what is kept most private? Now what crime is there, *I pray you, that is so much as kept secret among you, or is concealed by you? nay, what is there that is not open to your very enemies? for you show your transgressions after a pompous manner, and contend one with another which of you shall be more wicked than another; and you make a public demonstration of your injustice, as if it were virtue. However, there is a place left for your preservation, if you be willing to accept of it; and God is easily reconciled to those that confess their faults, and repent of them. O hard-hearted wretches as you are! cast away all your arms, and take pity of your country already going to ruin; return from your wicked ways, and have regard to the excellency of that city which you are going to betray, to that excellent temple with the donations of so many countries in it. Who could bear to be the first that should set that temple on fire? who could be willing that these things should be no more? and what is there that can better deserve to be preserved? O insensible creatures, and more stupid than are the stones themselves!* And if you cannot look at these things with discerning eyes, yet, however, have pity upon your families, and set before every one of your eyes your children, and wives, and parents, who will be gradually consumed either by famine or by war. I am sensible that this danger will extend to my mother, and wife, and to that family of mine who have been by no means ignoble, and indeed to one that hath been very eminent in old time; and perhaps you may imagine that it is on their account only that I give you this advice; if that be all, kill them; nay, take my own blood as a reward, if it may but procure your preservation; for I am ready to die, in case you will but return to a sound mind after my death.

This next passage speaks of the famine and the excessive pain people suffered from their hunger. I am reminded of Revelation 18:

21 Then a mighty angel picked up a boulder as large as a great millstone. He threw it into the ocean and shouted, "Babylon, the great city, will be thrown down as violently as I have thrown away this stone, and she will disappear forever. 22 Never again will the sound of music be heard there—no more harps, songs, flutes, or trumpets. There will be no industry of any kind, and no more milling of grain. 23 Her

nights will be dark, without a single lamp. There will be no happy voices of brides and grooms. This will happen because her merchants, who were the greatest in the world, deceived the nations with her sorceries. 24 In her streets the blood of the prophets was spilled. She was the one who slaughtered God's people all over the world."

Book V, Chapter X, Section 2

Intolerable Things Those That Stayed Behind Suffered By Famine

---

2. But as for the richer sort, it proved all one to them whether they staid in the city, or attempted to get out of it; for they were equally destroyed in both cases; for every such person was put to death under this pretense, that they were going to desert, but in reality that the robbers might get what they had. The madness of the seditious did also increase together with their famine, and both those miseries were every day inflamed more and more; for there was no corn which any where appeared publicly, but the robbers came running into, and searched men's private houses; and then, if they found any, they tormented them, because they had denied they had any; and if they found none, they tormented them worse, because they supposed they had more carefully concealed it. The indication they made use of whether they had any or not was taken from the bodies of these miserable wretches; which, if they were in good case, they supposed they were in no want at all of food; but if they were wasted away, they walked off without searching any further; nor did they think it proper to kill such as these, because they saw they would very soon die of themselves for want of food. Many there were indeed who sold what they had for one measure; it was of wheat, if they were of the richer sort; but of barley, if they were poorer. When these had so done, they shut themselves up in the inmost rooms of their houses, and ate the corn they had gotten; some did it without grinding it, by reason of the extremity of the want they were in, and others baked bread of it, according as necessity and fear dictated to them: a table was no where laid for a distinct meal, but

they snatched the bread out of the fire, half-baked, and ate it very hastily.

This next passage describes some pretty horrendous stuff. I am reminded here of the events leading to Jesus' crucifixion. Remember Matthew 27:

24 Pilate saw that he wasn't getting anywhere and that a riot was developing. So he sent for a bowl of water and washed his hands before the crowd, saying, "I am innocent of the blood of this man. The responsibility is yours!" 25 And all the people yelled back, "We will take responsibility for his death—we and our children!"

Book V, Chapter XI, Section 1

How The Jews Were Crucified Before the Walls of the City

---

1. So now Titus's banks were advanced a great way, notwithstanding his soldiers had been very much distressed from the wall. He then sent a party of horsemen, and ordered they should lay ambushes for those that went out into the valleys to gather food. Some of these were indeed fighting men, who were not contented with what they got by rapine; but the greater part of them were poor people, who were deterred from deserting by the concern they were under for their own relations; for they could not hope to escape away, together with their wives and children, without the knowledge of the seditious; nor could they think of leaving these relations to be slain by the robbers on their account; nay, the severity of the famine made them bold in thus going out; so nothing remained but that, when they were concealed from the robbers, they should be taken by the enemy; and when they were going to be taken, they were forced to defend themselves for fear of being punished; as after they had fought, they thought it too late to make any supplications for mercy; *so they were first whipped, and then tormented*

with all sorts of tortures, before they died, and were then crucified before the wall of the city. This miserable procedure made Titus greatly to pity them, while they caught every day five hundred Jews; nay, some days they caught more: yet it did not appear to be safe for him to let those that were taken by force go their way, and to set a guard over so many he saw would be to make such as great deal them useless to him. The main reason why he did not forbid that cruelty was this, that he hoped the Jews might perhaps yield at that sight, out of fear lest they might themselves afterwards be liable to the same cruel treatment. So the soldiers, out of the wrath and hatred they bore the Jews, nailed those they caught, one after one way, and another after another, to the crosses, by way of jest, when their multitude was so great, that room was wanting for the crosses, and crosses wanting for the bodies.

This next section highlights what Josephus believes to be the worst fate of any Jews. I am reminded of Jesus' words in Matthew 24:

21 For that will be a time of greater horror than anything the world has ever seen or will ever see again.

Book V, Chapter XIII, Section 4

The Great Slaughters and Sacrilege That Were in Jerusalem

---

4. Hereupon some of the deserters, having no other way, leaped down from the wall immediately, while others of them went out of the city with stones, as if they would fight them; but thereupon they fled away to the Romans. *But here a worse fate accompanied these than what they had found within the city; and they met with a quicker despatch from the too great abundance they had among the Romans, than they could have done from the famine among the Jews; for when they came first to the Romans, they were puffed up by the famine, and swelled like men in a*

dropsy; after which they all on the sudden overfilled those bodies that were before empty, and so burst asunder, excepting such only as were skillful enough to restrain their appetites, and by degrees took in their food into bodies unaccustomed thereto. Yet did another plague seize upon those that were thus preserved; for there was found among the Syrian deserters a certain person who was caught gathering pieces of gold out of the excrements of the Jews' bellies; for the deserters used to swallow such pieces of gold, as we told you before, when they came out, and for these did the seditious search them all; for there was a great quantity of gold in the city, insomuch that as much was now sold for twelve Attic, as was sold before for twenty-five. But when this contrivance was discovered in one instance, the fame of it filled their several camps, that the deserters came to them full of gold. So the multitude of the Arabians, with the Syrians, cut up those that came as supplicants, and searched their bellies. Nor does it seem to me that any misery befell the Jews that was more terrible than this, since in one night's time about two thousand of these deserters were thus dissected.

Josephus here describes the further torture the people were under in Jerusalem. He concludes that if Rome had not destroyed the Jews, their fate would have been sealed by a variety of other means.

Book V, Chapter XIII, Section 6

The Great Slaughters and Sacrilege That Were in Jerusalem

6. But as for John, when he could no longer plunder the people, he betook himself to sacrilege, and melted down many of the sacred utensils, which had been given to the temple; as also were many of those vessels which were necessary for such as ministered about holy things,—the caldrons, the dishes, and the table; nay, he did not abstain from those pouring-vessels that were sent them by Augustus and his wife; for the Romans emperors did ever both honour and adorn this temple: whereas this man, who was a Jew, seized upon what were the

donations of foreigners; and said to those that were with him, that it was proper for them to use divine things while they were fighting for the Divinity, without fear, and that such whose warfare is for the temple should live of the temple; on which account he emptied the vessels of that sacred wine and oil which the priests kept to be poured on the burnt-offerings, and which lay in the inner court of the temple, and distributed it among the multitude, who, in their anointing themselves and drinking, used above an hin of them; and here I cannot but speak my mind, and what the concerns I am under dictates to me, and it is this:—*I suppose that had the Romans made any longer delay in coming against these villains, the city would either have been swallowed up by the ground opening upon them, or been overflowed by water, or else been destroyed by such thunder as the country of Sodom perished by, for it had brought forth a generation of men much more atheistical that were those that suffered such punishments; for by their madness it was that all the people came to be destroyed.*

Notice here the numbers of the dead and the eating of excrement. Really bad times these were....

Book V, Chapter XIII, Section 7

The Great Slaughters And Sacrilege In Jerusalem

---

7. And, indeed, why do I relate these particular calamities? while Manneus, the son of Lazarus, came running to Titus at this very time, and told him that there had been carried out through that one gate, which was intrusted to his care, *no fewer than a hundred and fifteen thousand eight hundred and eighty dead bodies, in the interval between the fourteenth day of the month Xanthieus, when the Romans pitched their camp by the city, and the first day of the month Panemus.* This was itself a prodigious multitude; and though this man was not himself set as a governor at that gate, yet was he appointed to pay the public stipend for carrying these bodies out, and so was obliged of necessity to number

them, while the rest were buried by their relations; though all their burial was but this, to bring them away, and cast them out of the city. After this man there ran away to Titus many of the eminent citizens, and told him the entire number of the poor that were dead, and that no fewer than six hundred thousand were thrown out at the gates, though still the number of the rest could not be discovered; and they told him further, *that when they were no longer able to carry out the dead bodies of the poor, they laid their corpses on heaps in very large houses, and shut them up therein; as also that a medimnus of wheat was sold for a talent; and that when, a while afterward, it was not possible to gather herbs, by reason the city was all walled about, some persons were driven to that terrible distress as to search the common sewers and old dunghills of cattle, and to eat the dung which they got there; and what they of old could not endure so much as to see they now used for food. When the Romans barely heard all this, they commiserated their case; while the seditious, who saw it also, did not repent, but suffered the same distress to come upon themselves; for they were blinded by that fate which was already coming upon the city, and upon themselves also.*

This next section reflects on the fact that events still got worse. In fact, all of the trees of Judea had been cut down for battlements or for crucifixions.

Book VI, Chapter I, Section 1

The Desolate Nature Of Jerusalem And All Of Judea
That The Miseries Of The Jews Still Grew Worse

1. Thus did the miseries of Jerusalem grow worse and worse every day, and the seditious were still more irritated by the calamities they were under, even while the famine preyed upon themselves, after it had preyed upon the people. And indeed the multitude of carcases that lay in heaps one upon another was a horrible sight, and produced a pestilential stench, which was a hinderance to those that would make sallies

out of the city, and fight the enemy: but as those were to go in battle array, who had been already used to ten thousand murders, and must tread upon those dead bodies as they marched along, so were not they terrified, nor did they pity men as they marched over them: nor did they deem this affront offered to the deceased to be any ill omen to themselves; but as they had their right hands already polluted with the murders of their own countrymen, and in that condition ran out to fight with foreigners, they see to me to have cast a reproach upon God himself, as if he were too slow in punishing them; for the war was not now gone on with as if they had any hope of victory, for they gloried after a brutish manner in that despair of deliverance they were already in. And now the Romans, although they were greatly distressed in getting together their materials, raised their banks in on-and-twenty days, after they had cut down all the trees that were in the country that adjoined to the city, and that for ninety furlongs round about, as I have already related. *And truly the very view itself of the country was a melancholy thing; for those places which were before adorned with trees and pleasant gardens were now become a desolate country every way, and its trees were all cut down*: nor could any foreigner that had formerly seen Judea, and the most beautiful suburbs of the city, and now see it as a desert, but lament and mourn sadly at so great a change: for the was had laid all signs of beauty quite waste: nor, if any one that had known the place before had come on a sudden to it now, would have known it again; but though he were at the city itself, yet would he have inquired for it notwithstanding.

This section describes their "medical" techniques for continuing the fight.

Book VI, Chapter II, Section 9

Cutting Off of Infected Limbs

9. In the mean time, *the Jews were so distressed by the fights they had been in, as the war advanced higher and higher, and creeping up to the holy house itself, that they, as it were, cut off those limbs of their body which were infected, in order to prevent the distemper's spreading further;* for they set the north-west cloister, which was joined to the tower of Antonia, on fire, and after that brake off about twenty cubits of that cloister, and thereby made a beginning in burning the sanctuary; two days after which, or on the twenty-fourth day of the forenamed month, the Romans set fire to the cloister that joined to the other, when the fire went fifteen cubits farther. The Jews, in like manner, cut off its roof; nor did they entirely leave off what they were about till the tower of Antonia was parted from the temple, even when it was in their power to have stopped the fire; nay, they lay still while the temple was first set on fire, and deemed this spreading of the fire to be for their own advantage. However, the armies were still fighting one against another about the temple, and the war was managed by continual sallies of particular parties against one another.

This section relays the severity of the famine in Jerusalem. It is important to note these events to understand events that followed.

Book VI, Chapter III, Section 3

Another Description Of The Terrible Famine That Was In The City

3. Now of those that perished by famine in the city, the number was prodigious, and the miseries they underwent were unspeakable ; for if so much as the shadow of any kind of food did anywhere appear, a war was commenced presently; and the dearest friends fell a-fighting one with another about it, snatching from each other the most miserable supports of life. *Nor would men believe that those who were dying had no food; but the robbers would search them when they were expiring, lest any one should have concealed food in their bosoms, and counterfeited dying: nay, these robbers gaped for want, and ran about stumbling and staggering*

along like mad dogs, and reeling against the doors of the houses like drunken men; they would also, in the great distress they were in, rush into the very same houses two or three times in one and the same day. Moreover, their hunger was so intolerable, that it obliged them to chew everything, while they gathered such things as the most sordid animals would not touch, and endured to eat them; nor did they at length abstain from girdles and shoes; and the very leather which belonged to their shields they pulled off and gnawed : the very wisps of old hay became food to some; and some gathered up fibres, and sold a very small weight of them for four Attic. But why should I describe the shameless impudence that the famine brought on men in their eating inanimate things, while I am going to relate matter of fact, the like to which no history relates, either among the Greeks or Barbarians! It is horrible to speak of it, and incredible when heard. I had indeed willingly omitted this calamity of ours, that I might not seem to deliver what is so portentous to posterity, but that I have innumerable witnesses to it in my own age; and besides, my country would have had little reason to thank me for suppressing the miseries that she underwent at this time.

When I read the next two passages, I am reminded of Matthew 24:

19 How terrible it will be for pregnant women and for mothers nursing their babies in those days.

This pronouncement has an uncanny correspondence to the facts cited below. However, there is also a much more significant reference to these events in scripture. I ask you to read Deuteronomy 28 in its entirety before you read on here. Pay particular attention to this passage in its context:

53 The siege will be so severe that you will eat the flesh of your own sons and daughters, whom the LORD your God has given you. 54 The most tenderhearted man among you will have no compassion for his

own brother, his beloved wife, and his surviving children. 55 He will refuse to give them a share of the flesh he is devouring—the flesh of one of his own children—because he has nothing else to eat during the siege that your enemy will inflict on all your towns. 56 The most tender and delicate woman among you—so delicate she would not so much as touch her feet to the ground—will be cruel to the husband she loves and to her own son or daughter. 57 She will hide from them the afterbirth and the new baby she has borne, so that she herself can secretly eat them. She will have nothing else to eat during the siege and terrible distress that your enemy will inflict on all your towns.

Then, ask yourself if these events, and the others Josephus describes, match the events foretold in Deuteronomy and Matthew 24.

Book VI, Chapter III, Section 4

Another Description Of The Terrible Famine That Was In The City

4. Now there was a certain woman that dwelt beyond Jordan, her name was Mary; her father was Eleazar, of the village Bethezub, which signifies *the House of Hyssop*. She was eminent for her family and her wealth, and had fled away to Jerusalem with the rest of the multitude , and was with them besieged therein at this time. The other effects of this woman had been already seized upon; such I mean as she had brought with her out of Perea, and removed to the city. What she had treasured up besides, as also what food she had contrived to save, had also been carried off by the rapacious guards, who came every day running into her house for that purpose. This put the poor woman into a very great passion, and by the frequent reproaches and imprecations she cast at these rapacious villains, she had provoked them to anger against her; but none of them, either out of the indignation she had raised against herself, or out of the commiseration of her case, would take away her life; and if she found any food, she perceived her labours

were for others, and not for herself; and it was now become impossible for her any way to find any more food, while the famine pierced through her very bowels and marrow, when also her passion was fired to a degree beyond the famine itself: nor did she consult with anything but with her passion and the necessity she was in. She then attempted a most unnatural thing; and snatching up her son, who was a child sucking at her breast, she said, "O thou miserable infant! for whom shall I preserve thee in this war, this famine, and this sedition ? As to the war with the Romans, if they preserve our lives, we must be slaves! The famine also will destroy us, even before that slavery comes upon us; yet are these seditious rogues more terrible than both the other. Come on; be thou my food, and be thou a fury to these seditious varlets and a byeword to the world, which is all that is now wanting to complete the calamities of us Jews." As soon as she had said this, she slew her son; and then roasted him, and ate one half of him, and kept the other half by her concealed. Upon this the seditious come in presently, and smelling the horrid scent of this food, they threatened her that they would cut her throat immediately if she did not shew them what food she had gotten ready. She replied, that she had saved a very fine portion of it for them; and withal uncovered what was left of her son. Hereupon they were seized with a horror and amazement of mind, and stood astonished at the sight; when she said to them "This is mine own son; and what hath been done was mine own doing! Come, eat of this food; for I have eaten of it myself! Do not you pretend to be either more tender than a woman, or more compassionate than a mother; but if you be so scrupulous, and do abominate this my sacrifice, as I have eaten the one half, let the rest be reserved for me also." After which, those men went out trembling, being never so much affrighted at anything as they were at this, and with some difficulty they left the rest of that meat to the mother. Upon which, the whole city was full of horrid action immediately; and while everyone laid this miserable case before their own eyes, they trembled, as if this unheard-of-action had been done by themselves. So those that were thus distressed by the famine were very desirous to die (1); and those already dead were esteemed happy, because they had not live long enough either to hear or see such miseries.

Book VI, Chapter V, Section 1

The Great Distress The Jews Were In Upon The Conflagration Of The Holy House

---

1. While the holy house was on fire, everything was plundered that came to hand, and ten thousand of those that were caught were slain; nor was there a commiseration of any age, or any reverence of gravity; but children, and old men, and profane persons, and priests, were all slain in the same manner; so that this war went round all sorts of men, and brought them to destruction, and as well those that made supplication for their lives, as those that defended themselves by fighting. The flame was also carried a long way, and made an echo, together with the groans of those that were slain; and because this hill was high, and the works at the temple were very great, one would have thought that the whole city had been on fire. *Nor can one imagine anything either greater or more terrible than this noise; for there was at once a shout of the Roman legions, who were marching all together, and a sad clamour of the seditious, who were now surrounded with fire and sword. The people also that were left above were beaten back upon the enemy, and under a great consternation, and made sad moans at the calamity they were under; the multitude also that was in the city joined in this outcry with those that were upon the hill; and besides many of those that were worn away by the famine, and their mouths almost closed when they saw the fire of the holy house, they exerted their utmost strength, and brake out into groans and outcries again: Perea did also return he echo, as well as the mountains round about, and augmented the force of the entire noise. Yet was the misery itself more terrible than this disorder; for one would have thought that the hill itself, on which the temple stood, was seething-hot, as full of fire on every part of it, that the blood was larger in quantity than the fire, and those that were slain more in number that those that slew them; for the ground did nowhere appear visible, for the dead bodies that lay on it; but the soldiers*

went over the heaps of these bodies, as they ran upon such as fled from them.

And now it was that the multitude of the robbers were thrust out by the Romans, and had much ado to get into the outer court, and from thence into the city, while the remainder of the populace fled into the cloister of that outer court. As for the priests, some of them plucked up from the holy house the spikes that were upon it, with their bases, which were made of lead, and shot them at the Romans instead of darts. But then as they gained nothing by so doing, and as the fire burst out upon them, they retired to the wall that was eight cubits broad, and there they tarried; yet did two of these of eminence among them, who might have saved themselves by going over to the Romans, or have borne up with courage, and taken their fortune with the others, throw themselves into the fire, and were burnt together with the holy house; their names were Merius to son of Belgas, and Joseph the son of Daleus.

Note the presence and effect of another false prophet and the others who led to such destruction (Matthew 24:24):

Book VI, Chapter V, Section 2

Concerning A False Prophet

2. And now the Romans, judging that it was in vain to spare what was round the holy house, burnt all those places, as also the remains of the cloisters and the gates, two excepted; the one on the east side, and the other on the south; both which, however, they burnt afterward. They also burnt down the treasury-chambers, in which was an immense quantity of money, and an immense number of garments, and other precious goods, there reposited; and, to speak all in a few words, there it was that the entire riches of the Jews were heaped up together, while the rich people had there built themselves chambers. The soldiers also

came to the rest of the cloisters that were in the outer temple, whither the women and children and a great mixed multitude of the people fled, in number about six thousand. But before Caesar had determined anything about these people, or given the commanders any orders relating to them, the soldiers were in such a rage, that they set the cloister of fire; by which means it came to pass that some of these were destroyed by throwing themselves down headlong, and some were burnt in the cloisters themselves. Nor did any one of these escape with his life.

A false prophet was the occasion of these people's destruction, who had made a public proclamation in the city that very day, that God commanded them to get up upon the temple, and that there they should receive miraculous signs of their deliverance. Now, there was then a great number of false prophets suborned by the tyrants to impose upon the people, who denounced this to them, that they should wait for deliverance from God; and this was in order to keep them from deserting, and that they might be buoyed up above fear and care by such hopes. Now, a man that is in adversity does easily comply with such promises; for when such a seducer makes him believe that he shall be delivered from those miseries which oppress him, then it is that the patient is full of hopes of such deliverance.

This next section is perhaps the most astounding and difficult to believe. Josephus documents some very significant signs which he claims to have preceded the destruction. Keep in mind, he is a Jewish historian with presumably no knowledge of Jesus Christ's prophecy in Matthew 24. Specifically, I ask you to consider this portion:

30 And then at last, the sign of the coming of the Son of Man will appear in the heavens, and there will be deep mourning among all the

nations of the earth. And they will see the Son of Man arrive on the clouds of heaven with power and great glory.

The sign that preceded Jesus' birth was a star over Bethlehem. "The sign" of His coming was a star over the town. Now, look at the sign seen over Jerusalem, and the other amazing signs he documents here:

Book VI, Chapter 5, Section 3

The Signs That Preceded The Destruction

---

3. Thus were the miserable people persuaded by these deceivers, and such as belied God himself; while they did not attend, nor give credit, to the signs that were so evident, and did so plainly foretell their future desolation; but, like men infatuated, without either eyes to see or minds to consider, did not regard the denunciations that God made to them. *Thus there was a star resembling a sword, which stood over the city, and a comet, that continued a whole year.* Thus also, before the Jews' rebellion, and before those commotions which preceded the war, when the people were come in great crowds to the feast of unleavened bread, on the eight day of the month Xanthicus, and at the ninth hour of the night, so great a light shone round the altar and the holy house, that it appeared to be bright day-time; which light lasted for half an hour. This light seemed to be a good sign to the unskilful, but was so interpreted by the sacred scribes as to portend those events that followed immediately upon it.

At the same festival also, a heifer, as she was led by the high priest to be sacrificed, brought forth a lamb in the midst of the temple. Moreover, the eastern gate of the inner which was of brass, and vastly heavy, and had been with difficulty shut by twenty men, and rested upon a basis armed with iron, and had bolts fastened very deep into the firm floor, which was there made of one entire stone, was seen to be opened of its own accord about the sixth hour of the night. Now, those that kept watch in the temple came thereupon running to the captain of the temple, and told him of it; who then came up thither, and not without great difficulty was able to shut the gate again. This also appeared to the vulgar to be a very happy prodigy, as if God did thereby open them the gate of happiness. But the men of learning understood it, that the security of their holy house was dissolved of its own accord, and that the gate was opened for the advantage of their enemies. So these publicly declared, that this signal forshewed the desolation that was coming upon them.

Besides these, a few days after that feast, on the one-and-twentieth day of the month Artemisius, a certain prodigious and incredible phenomenon appeared; I suppose the account of it would seem to be a fable, were it not related by those that saw it, and were not the events that followed it of so considerable a nature as to deserve such signals; for, before sun-setting, chariots and troops of soldiers in their armour were seen running about among the clouds, and surrounding of cities. Moreover, at that feast which we call Pentecost, as the priests were going by night into the inner [court of the] temple, as their custom was, to perform their sacred ministrations, they said that, in the first place, they felt a quaking, and heard a great noise, and after that they heard a sound as of a great multitude, saying, "Let us remove hence."

But, what is still more terrible, there was one Jesus, the son of Ananus, a plebeian, and an husbandman, who, four years before the war began, and at a time when the city was in very great peace and prosperity, came to that feast whereon it is our custom for every one to make tabernacles to God in the temple, began on a sudden to cry aloud, "A voice from the east, a voice from the west, a voice from the four winds, a voice against Jerusalem and the holy house, a voice against the bridegrooms and the brides, and a voice against this whole people!" This was his cry, as he went about by day and by night, in all the lanes of the city. However, certain of the most eminent among the populace had great indignation at this dire cry of his, and took up the man, and gave him a great number of severe stripes; yet did not he either say anything for himself, or anything peculiar to those that chastised him, but still he went on with the same words which he cried before. Hereupon our rulers supposing, as the case proved to be, that this was a sort of divine fury in the man, brought him to the Roman procurator—where he was whipped till his bones were laid bare; yet did he not make any supplication for himself, nor shed any tears, but turning his voice to the most lamentable tone possible, at every stroke of the whip his answer was , "Woe, woe to Jerusalem!" And when Albinus (for he was then our procurator) asked him, Who he was? and whence he came? and why he uttered such words? he made no manner of reply to what he said, but still did not leave off his melancholy ditty, till Albinus took him to be a madman, and dismissed him. Now, during all the time that passed before the war began, this man did not go near any of the citizens, nor was seen by them while he said so; but he every day uttered these lamentable words, as if it were his premeditated vow, "Woe, woe to Jerusalem!" Nor did he give ill words to any of those that beat him every day, nor good words to those that gave him food; but this was his reply to all men, and indeed no other than a melancholy presage of what was to come. This cry of his was the loudest at the festivals; and he continued this ditty for seven years and five months, without growing hoarse, or being tired therewith, until the very time that he saw his presage in earnest fulfilled in our siege, when it ceased; for, as he was going round upon the wall, he cried out with his utmost force, "Woe, woe to the city again, and to the people, and to the holy house!" And just as he added at the last—"Woe, woe to myself also!" there came a stone out of one of the engines, and smote him, and killed him immediately: and as he was uttering the very same presages, he gave up the ghost.

In this next section, note the numbers of dead and captured.

Book VI, Chapter IX, Section 3

The Number Of Captives, And Of Those That Perished In The Siege.

3. Now the number of those that were carried captive during the whole war was collected to be ninety-seven thousand; as was the number of those that perished during the whole siege, eleven hundred thousand, the greater part of whom were indeed of the same nation, but not belonging to the city itself; for they were come up from all the country to the feast of unleavened bread, and were on a sudden shut up by an army, which, at the very first, occasioned so great a straitness among them, that there came a pestilential destruction upon them, and soon afterward such a famine as destroyed them more suddenly. And that this city could contain so many people in it is manifest by that number of them which was taken under Cestius, who being desirous of informing Nero of the power of the city, who otherwise was disposed to contemn that nation, entreated the high priests, if the thing were possible, to take the number of their whole multitude. So these high priests, upon the coming of their feast which is called the Passover, when they slay their sacrifices, from the ninth hour to the eleventh, but so that a company not less than belong to every sacrifice, (for it is not lawful for them to feast singly by themselves,) and many of us are twenty in a company, found the number of sacrifices was two hundred and fifty-six thousand five hundred; which, upon the allowance of no more than ten that feast together, amounts to two millions seven hundred thousand and two hundred persons that were pure and holy; for as to those that have the leprosy, or the gonorrhea, or women that have their monthly courses, or such as are otherwise polluted, it is not lawful for them to be partakers of this sacrifice; nor indeed for any foreigners neither, who come hither to worship.

Note here the account of the history of Jerusalem:

Book VI, Chapter X, Section 1

That Whereas The City Of Jerusalem Had Been [Six] Times Taken Formerly, This Was The Second Time Of Its Desolation. A Brief Account Of Its History

---

1. And thus was Jerusalem taken, in the second year of the reign of Vespasian, on the eight day of the month Gorpieus. It had been taken five times before, though this was the second time of its desolation ; for Shishak, the king of Egypt, and after his Antiochus, and after him Pompey, and after him Sosius and Herod took the city, but still preserved it; but before all these, the king of Babylon conquered it, and made it desolate, one thousand four hundred and sixty-eight years and six months after it was built. But he who first built it was a potent man among the Canaanites, and is in our tongue called the Righteous King, for such he really was; on which account he was the first priest of God, and first built a temple, and called the city Jerusalem, which was formerly called Salem. However, David, the king of the Jews, ejected the Canaanites, and settled his own people therein. It was demolished entirely by the Babylonians, four hundred and seventy-seven years and six months after him. And from king David, who was the first of the Jews who reigned therein, to this destruction under Titus, were one thousand one hundred and seventy-nine years; but from its first building, till this last destruction, were two thousand one hundred and seventy-seven years; yet hath not its great antiquity, nor its vast riches, nor the diffusion of its nation over all the habitable earth, nor the greatness of the veneration paid to it on a religious account, been sufficient to preserve it from being destroyed. And thus ended the siege of Jerusalem.

Remember Matthew 24:

2 But he told them, "Do you see all these buildings? I assure you, they will be so completely demolished that not one stone will be left on top of another!"

Book VII, Chapter I, Section 1

The Entire City Of Jerusalem Was Demolished, Excepting Three Towers

---

1. Now as soon as the army had no more people to slay or to plunder, because there remained none to be the objects of their fury, (for they would not have spared any, had there remained any other work to be done,) Caesar gave orders that they should now demolish the entire city and temple, but should leave as many of the towers standing as were of the greatest eminency; that is, Phasaelus, and Hippicus, and Mariamne; and so much of the wall as enclosed the city on the west side. This wall was spared, in order to afford a camp for such as were to lie in garrison, as were the towers also spared, *in order to demonstrate to posterity what kind of city it was, and how well fortified, which the Roman valor had subdued; but for all the rest of the wall, it was so thoroughly laid even with the ground by those that dug it up to the foundation, that there was left nothing to make those that came thither believe it had ever been inhabited. This was the end which Jerusalem came to by the madness of those that were for innovations; a city otherwise of great magnificence, and of mighty fame among all mankind.*

Book VII, Chapter 8, Section 7

Jerusalem Was Demolished to the Very Foundations

Where is this city that was believed to have God himself inhabiting therein? *It is now demolished to the very foundations, and hath nothing but that monument of it preserved, I mean the camp of those that hath destroyed it, which still dwells upon its ruins; some unfortunate old men also lie upon the ashes of the temple, and a few women are there preserved alive by the enemy, for our bitter shame and reproach.* Now who is there that revolves these things in his mind, and yet is able to bear the sight of the sun, though he might live out of danger? Who is there so much his country's enemy, or so unmanly, and so desirous of living, as not to repent that he is still alive? And I cannot but wish that we had all died before we had seen that holy city demolished by the hands of our enemies, or the foundations of our holy temple dug up after so profane a manner.

This account of Josephus concludes the portion of the appendix. In the next volume, I'll site some other historians on their views of these events. The Josephus citations relay the distinct reality of Jesus Christ's words in Matthew 24 coming to fruition in 63-70 A.D. Study these well, because it forms an important construct for understanding eschatology.

About the Author

Tim Kirk is an officer in the United States Air Force. He serves as an associate staffer with the Navigators Military Ministry, and leads a small assembly of disciples in the area near his home in Georgia. He hails from Norman, Oklahoma, and from his parent's home in Victorville, California. Tim is very proud of his parents, Dr. Robert and Vicki Kirk, who led the family to California after providing Tim a Godly upbringing in the "Holy Land" of the Sooners. His brother, Mark, and he graduated from Hesperia High School in California. Tim defers to his smarter brother, who was Valedictorian of his class, and is a career educator.

Tim is a 1993 graduate of the United States Air Force Academy in Colorado Springs, Colorado. There he earned a Bachelor of Science in Biology with a minor in German language. After graduation, he was commissioned as a Second Lieutenant in the U.S. Air Force, graduated from the Aircraft Maintenance and Munitions Officer Course, and became an aircraft maintenance officer. His graduate education includes a professional certification as a military contracting officer, and he will graduate in July of 2002 with a Masters degree in Sports Medicine from the U.S. Sports Academy in Daphne, AL.

His ministry includes evangelism, making disciples, and the study of theology. His emphasis is on developing in himself and others spiritual fruit: a love for God intellectually and behaviorally, and a love for others. His motto for his life and discipleship is, "In essentials, unity; in non-essentials, liberty; in all things, charity."

His wife, Catherine, and he live together with their four birds and two bunny rabbits. Catherine is an elementary school teacher with a Bachelors degree in Education. They are avid sport enthusiasts, participating in regular trips to the base gym, mountain hiking and biking, and snow skiing at any opportunity. Tim also enjoys helping out at wrestling practice at the local high school from time to time. They are members of the "Highpointers" club; their goal is to eventually reach the highest point of each of the 50 states. So far, they have reached 15 of them together.

Tim is also a technophile, with a strong interest in computer technology. He favors Apple Macintosh computers, and considers himself a "Mac Evangelist." He has worked to help Apple promote Macs, earning the distinction of Apple Product Professional for three consecutive years. Rumor has it he secretly owns a PC as well as a Mac, but this remains unconfirmed. Another hobby he pursues is working security for the NFL. He is a licensed security officer, and served in Super Bowls XXXV and XXXVI.

He writes in his spare time, and enjoys research, bible study, and conversations about spiritual things. He can be reached at his email: **cap10krk@mac.com** for comments and suggestions.

Titles by the Author in the IW2BLB Series

1. <u>I Want to be "Left Behind"</u>—An examination of the ideas behind the popular series and the "end times."

2. <u>Facts About the "Tribulation Force" Me to Reconsider</u>—An Historical analysis of Josephus and the events leading up to the destruction of Jerusalem.

3. <u>Where in the World is "Nicolae?"</u>—A Study of the scriptural "beast," "antichrist," and the "man of lawlessness."

4. <u>What did Peter and Paul Think About the "Soul Harvest?"</u>—A Study of the apostles' view of the "end times."

5. <u>Watch Out for Textual "Assassins"</u>—A Study of the principles of interpretation, both literal and "literal."

6. <u>A Cube with 6 Sides Does Not "Apolyon" Make</u>—A Study of the historical facts about the apostles, the tribes of Israel, and the church in John's Revelation.

7. <u>"The Indwelling" of a Commentary, a Chart, and a Pyramid</u>—A Study of modern premillennial views and their origins in history.

8. <u>Can Anyone Remember "The Mark" in Exodus?</u>—An Examination of scriptural uses of "marks" in OT and NT scripture, and significance in history and prophecy.

9. <u>Memoirs of a Summer "Desecration"</u>—A Study of the historical facts about the destruction of Jerusalem in 70 AD.

10. "The Remnant" of Reason—A Study of the Revelation of John, its date of authorship, and its relationship to the rest of scripture.

0-595-22427-X